french bu

C000216273

understanding and
caring for your breed

Written by
Jennifer Watson

french bulldog

understanding and
caring for your breed

Written by
Jennifer Watson

Pet Book Publishing Company

The Old Hen House, St Martin's Farm, Zeals, BA12 6NZ, United Kingdom.

Printed and bound in South Korea.

All rights reserved. No part of this work may be reproduced, in any form or by any means, electronic or mechanical, including photocopying, recording or by any information storage and retrieval system, without the prior written permission of the publisher.

Copyright © Pet Book Publishing Company 2015.

Every reasonable care has been taken in the compilation of this publication. The Publisher and Author cannot accept liability for any loss, damage, injury or death resulting from the keeping of French Bulldogs by user(s) of this publication, or from the use of any materials, equipment, methods or information recommended in this publication or from any errors or omissions that may be found in the text of this publication or that may occur at a future date, except as expressly provided by law.

The 'he' pronoun is used throughout this book instead of the rather impersonal 'it', however no gender bias is intended.

ISBN: 978-1-910488-20-1

Acknowledgements

The publishers would like to thank the following for help with photography: Janet and David Furneaux (Dajan); Lucy Bonsall (Mugg Shots); Bill and Joe Blacker (Crossguns); Penny Rankine- Parsons (Penburton); Paul Pearce (Helena); Philip and Alyson Stemp (Laudmell)

Contents

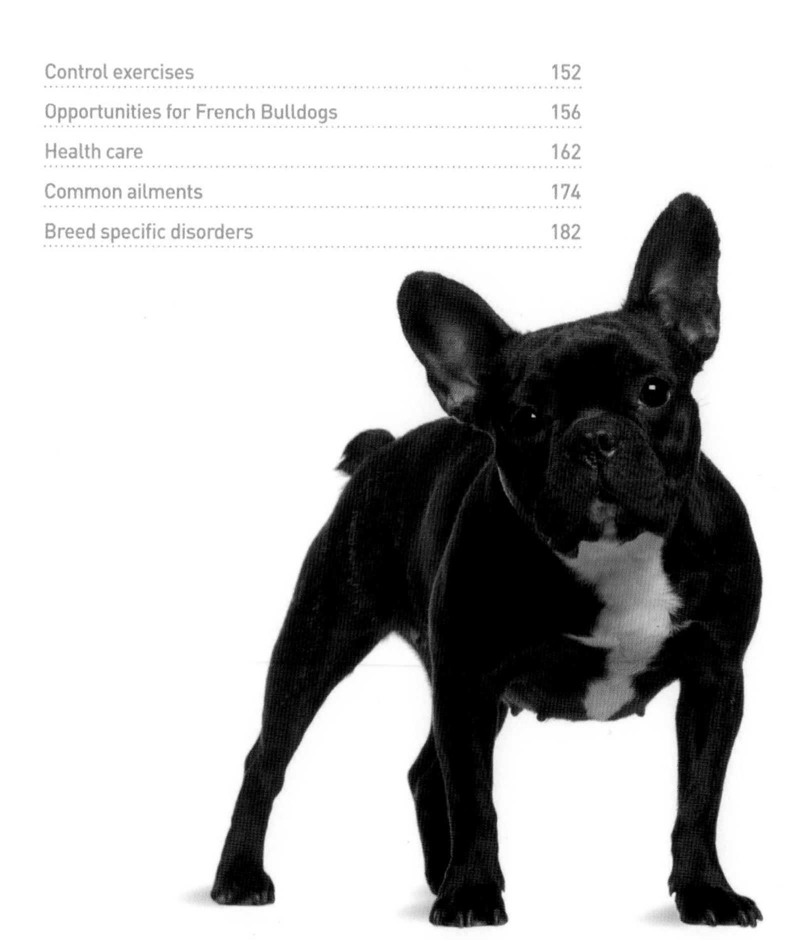

Introducing the French Bulldog

Cheeky, affectionate and a born entertainer, the French Bulldog is the perfect pet for many families. Highly adaptable, he will fit in with lots of different lifestyles, and his unique Bulldog looks will mean he always stands out in a crowd.

Physical characteristics

Bred down from the larger English Bulldog, the Frenchie is, in essence, a Bulldog in miniature.

He has the typical Bulldog expression which comes from the short muzzle, the flat, upturned nose and the undershot jaw. This gives him a pugnacious expression, but it is softened by his round, dark eyes which

convey huge interest in everything that is going on. The Frenchie's bat ears, which are carried parallel and upright, are a breed speciality, and mark a divergence from the larger Bulldog, which has rose-shaped ears.

Hugely expressive, the position of the ears will tell you exactly how your Frenchie is feeling which, typically, ranges between alert, playful, loving and on the lookout for mischief!

As the Frenchie has a very short tail, he cannot signal his feelings with his tail carriage, which is a common means of communication in other breeds. Most owners reckon that the Frenchie has more than made up for this with the unique way he uses his ears.

The French Bulldog has a powerful, muscular body, and is heavy for his size. However, he should be active and move freely, and will delight you with his sudden, unexpected bursts of energy.

The coat is short, smooth and easy to care for, and you have a choice of colours. Frenchies can be all shades of fawn, brindle and pied.

Temperament

Where to start? The French Bulldog has the most wonderful temperament, and although they share many outstanding characteristics, you will find that every Frenchie is very much an individual. The Breed Standard, which describes what to look for in a French Bulldog, uses a variety of adjectives to describe the Frenchie temperament, and these warrant further investigation.

- Courageous: The old style English Bulldog was a fighting dog that was pitched against a tethered bull – a huge animal in comparison – so remarkable courage was a necessity. The Frenchie has inherited his ancestor's fearless approach to life.

The Frenchie is a fun-loving dog that will give you endless entertainment.

- Clown-like: What a brilliant combination to be courageous and yet clown-like! This is pure French Bulldog – he will take on the world, and make you laugh at the same time...
- Vivacious: This sums up the breed's essential *joie de vivre.*
- Deeply affectionate: The Frenchie is a most loving dog who adores his human family. The American Breed Standard describes the French Bulldog as being an adaptable and comfortable companion with an even disposition . This underlines how easy it is to live with a Frenchie.
- Sociable: The Frenchie gets on well with virtually everyone he comes across, be they human, canine or feline.
- Playful: Many breeds lose their playfulness as they grow older. Not so the Frenchie, who will give you endless entertainment as he interacts with all members of his family pack, and as he goes about his daily life.
- Intelligent: He may not be a star performer in canine sports, but there is no doubting the Frenchie's mental aptitude. He is a thinking dog that can show great sensitivity.

The ideal home

The Frenchie is a convenient size and has the adaptable nature that means all homes are pretty much the same to him. He will fit into a small apartment and will be equally content in a larger home.

He is well suited to urban living, but he will also enjoy country pursuits. He is a brilliant playmate if you have a young family, but he will also be a loving companion in a quieter household.

In terms of exercise, the Frenchie is equally adaptable. He will be content with very little, particularly if it is raining... Persuading a Frenchie to go out when it is wet is quite an undertaking, which shows what sensible dogs they are!

If you are more active, a Frenchie will enjoy leisurely expeditions, but he is not built for endurance and should never be over-exercised in hot weather (see page 180).

Basically, the French Bulldog is a natural when it comes to fitting in – all he asks is to be given lots of love, lots of attention, and to be included in all family activities.

Tracing back in time

The Bulldog is a quintessentially British dog with his pugnacious appearance and steadfast character, summing up the spirit of the nation. Then you add in a French connection, and the result is a unique breed combining power with grace, and producing a dog with a courageous yet loving temperament.

To trace the history of the French Bulldog you must first go back to his ancestor, the English Bulldog. This was a dog that was lighter in build and longer in the leg than the Bulldog we know today, as his primary role was as a fighting dog.

For centuries bull baiting was a national pastime in England where crowds of spectators would watch the spectacle of a Bulldog being pitched against a tethered bull.

But by the late 1700s, the fast and furious 'sport' of dog fighting was all the rage. A more agile dog was needed, and so Bulldogs were crossed with lightweight, feisty terriers, and the old style Bulldog started to dwindle in numbers. When the Humane Act of 1835 outlawed bull baiting and dog fighting, the breeding of Bulldogs ceased to the point where the breed almost disappeared.

Fortunately it was saved from total extinction by a dedicated band of breeders who focused on reducing the Bulldog's size and modifying his pugnacious character so that he would find a new role as family companion.

French connection

Small size Bulldogs grew in popularity, and were a favourite among working class families. The lace makers of Nottingham seemed to have a particular affection for the new style breed, and when families migrated to Normandy in France, searching for work, they took their dogs with them. Not only were the mini Bulldogs small enough to fit into the cramped accommodation allocated to workers, they were also efficient rat catchers.

In time they were adopted by the local French population and, interestingly, became the favourites of street traders, publicans and prostitutes.

The upper classes were also attracted by their unique looks and affectionate character, and ladies were seen carrying their miniature Bulldogs as they promenaded in fashionable quarters of Paris.

As demand grew, eagle-eyed breeders spotted an opportunity and travelled to England to see if they could buy up small size Bulldogs. Trade increased rapidly during the 1870s and 1880s and as a consequence they became scarce in England while they flourished in France.

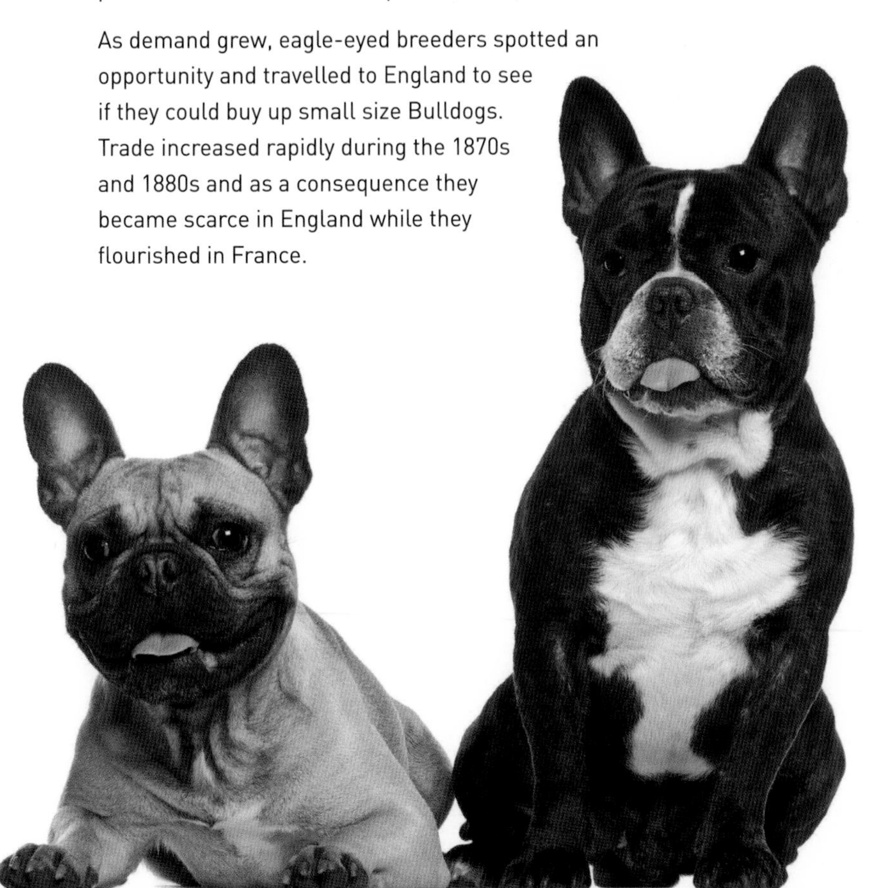

Developing the breed

Dog breeders have deep passions, and this often leads to controversy. So it was with the miniaturised Bulldog and at the end of the 19th century a split developed over what the new 'breed' should really look like.

Britain had taken a back seat in the development of the small size Bulldogs, but this was all to change when George Krehl imported six small Bulldogs from Paris in 1893. He was a Bulldog breeder and he believed that the French dogs would infuse quality into his bloodlines.

Reaction to the French imports was mixed; some fanciers felt they would pollute English lines, but there were also a strong band of admirers who were anxious to promote the new 'Toy Bulldogs'.

The Kennel Club in England set up a separate classification in the Stud Book for Toy Bulldogs, and in 1898 the Toy Bulldog Club was established with the aim of breeding pure Toy Bulldogs which resembled the original Bulldog as closely as possible, in everything but size. The desired weight was below 9kg (20lb), and ears were to be rose-shaped, although tulip-shaped ears were allowed.

The big divide

French breeders were not impressed with developments in England. They were adamant that bat ears had to be a distinguishing feature of the new breed, and rejected rose-eared dogs from their breeding programmes.

Controversy raged, and a split became inevitable. Fanciers of French-bred Bulldogs with bat ears decided the only option was to break away from the Toy Bulldog Club and form their own club. The French Bulldog Club of England was established, and they adopted a Breed Standard (a written description of the breed) which was virtually identical to the Standard that had been drawn up in France.

The new club held its first show in 1903 and Monsieur Menans de Corre, president of the Club du Bouledogue Francais, was invited to judge the 51 entries.

As the new breed grew in popularity, so the Toy Bulldog lost its following and by 1914, it had disappeared

Frenchies in the USA

The first small-size Bulldogs to arrive in the USA were a mixture of types imported from Europe in the late 19th century. Bred down from larger Bulldogs, both rose ears and bat ears were considered acceptable.

Bat-shaped ears were viewed as a defining feature of the breed.

But American breeders kept close tabs on what was happening in France, and when the French Bull Dog Club of America was founded in 1897, they adopted the French Standard and from then onwards they bred exclusively for bat-eared dogs.

Development and refinement of the breed progressed, with the most significant advances being made in the second half of the 20th century. Colour is the most notable difference between European and American-bred dogs, with a prevalence of cream dogs, without a black mask, in the USA. In fact, we have the Americans to thank for the inclusion of the fawn colour; it was originally rejected by European and English breeders as being too reminiscent of the Toy Bulldog, but it has always been allowed in the USA.

It was not until the 1950s that fawns were universally accepted, and there is still an issue with the inclusion of fawn pieds. Again, this colour has always been accepted in the USA. Europe decided to include it in the 1990s, but the UK is still holding out. To date, brindle pieds remain the only accepted pied colour that is shown in British show rings.

The international Frenchie

Fawn coloured Frenchies have always been popular in the USA.

Today the French Bulldog is well established as a breed and its popularity is growing in the modern era where a small-sized, adaptable dog is a prerequisite for many families.

Initially France was the major source of exports as the breed spread further afield but now the gene base is truly international, with dogs from the UK Austria, Germany, Holland, and the USA all making a major impact on the breed.

What should a French Bulldog look like?

The French Bulldog with his compact, muscular body, short face, snub nose and spectacular bat ears, is a striking sight. So what should the perfect Frenchie look like?

The aim of breeders is to produce dogs that are sound healthy, typical examples of their chosen breed, in terms of both looks and temperament. To achieve this, they are guided by a Breed Standard, which is a written blueprint describing the perfect specimen. Of course, there is no such thing as a 'perfect' dog, but breeders aspire to produce dogs that conform as closely as possible to the picture in words presented by the Breed Standard. In the show ring, judges use the Breed Standard to assess the dogs that come before them, and it is the dog that, in their opinion,

comes closest to the ideal, that will win top honours.

This has significance beyond the sport of showing, for it is the dogs that win in the ring which will be used for breeding. The winners of today are therefore responsible for passing on their genes to future generations and preserving the breed in its best form.

There are some differences in the wording of the Breed Standard depending on national kennel clubs; the American Kennel Club and the Federation Cynologique Internationale, which is the governing body for 86 countries, have far more descriptive Standards than the brief outline given in the English version, and there is also a significant difference regarding colour.

General appearance

This is a small, sturdy dog, powerful for his size with heavy bone, yet still remaining active. No point should be exaggerated and overall balance should be considered essential. Males and females should be instantly identifiable.

Temperament

The Frenchie is a joy to live with; he is sociable and adaptable, and shows deep affection for his family.

He is also intelligent, can be courageous, and as bonus, he loves to play the clown!

Head and skull

The French Bulldog is known as a 'head breed', meaning that the utmost importance is placed on this feature. It should be relatively large in order to be in balance with the powerful neck and sturdy body. The first impression is one of squareness; if you measure from the top of the skull to the chin, and then from the outer points of the cheekbones, the distance should be pretty much the same.

The skull should be flat between the ears, with a domed forehead. The skin should allow for fine wrinkling when the dog is alert. The muzzle is broad and the stop (the step up between the muzzle and the forehead) is well defined. Typical of brachycephalic breeds, the nose is short and upturned, but it is emphasised that the nostrils should be open and well developed to allow for normal breathing. The lower jaw is deep and square and is slightly undershot. Nose and lips should be black.

Eyes

Preferably dark in colour, the eyes should be set relatively wide apart on the same level as the stop.

They are round in shape, and although they often appear prominent, this exaggeration is discouraged. When a dog is looking forward, no white of eye should be visible.

Ears

The French Bulldog's bat ears are very much a feature of the breed.

They are set high on the head, but should not be too close together. In terms of shape, they are broad at the base and rounded at the top. The Frenchie carries his ears erect, and the skin of the ears should be fine and soft to the touch.

Mouth

The conformation of the jaw is slightly undershot which means that when the mouth is closed the lower teeth come in front of the upper teeth. As the Frenchie has very broad jaws, both upper and lower canine teeth (the pointed, conical teeth sometimes known as 'fangs') are set wider apart than in other dogs of similar size.

Neck

The neck is an important feature in achieving the correct balance in conformation. It needs to be sufficiently strong and thickset to join the large head to a short, compact body. It also needs to be long enough to form a graceful, well-muscled arch to give the impression of strength.

There is a small amount of loose skin (dewlap) at the lower jawline, but the underline of the neck should give a clean outline.

The short muzzle and upturned nose are typical features of brachycephalic breeds.

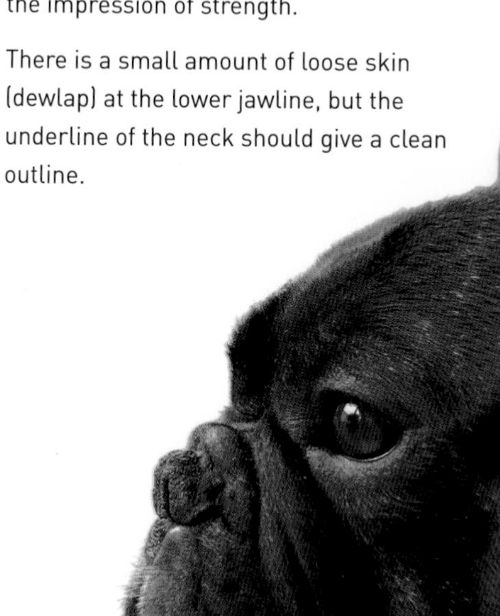

Forequarters

The front legs are short, muscular and straight. It is very important that they are set wide apart to give a powerful front, with the chest well let down between the two legs. The shoulders are short, thick and muscled; the elbows are held close to the body.

Body

The French Bulldog has a slightly 'roached' back. This means there should be a very slight fall to the back between the shoulders; the spine then rises to form a gentle, gradual curve to the point of the tail. The body itself should be short and well rounded. It should be broader at the shoulders and narrow slightly beyond the ribs. The overall impression should be compact and powerful.

Hindquarters

The hind legs are strong and muscular. They are slightly longer than the front legs which has the effect of slightly elevating the hindquarters. The hock joint (the ankle) should not be too angulated.

Tail

The Frenchie has a natural short, undocked tail, which is set on low. It is thick at the root and tapers to the tip. Ideally, it should have sufficient length to cover the anus. Tails with minor kinks are acceptable, but a tail that is tightly clamped to the rear, or one that turns in towards the body is undesirable, as it increases the risk of infection.

Coat

The Frenchie has a smooth coat, which is fine in texture. The skin is soft and loose, especially at the head and shoulders, and forms wrinkles.

Colour

The colours are brindle, pied and fawn.

Fawn: Shades can range from cream to red.

Brindle: A pattern of stripes overlying the fawn shades. A white chest is perfectly acceptable, but further white markings, such as on the face, legs and back of the neck, are not desirable.

Pied: White should always predominate; brindle patches do not need to be symmetrical. In the USA and countries governed by the Federation Internationale Cynologique (FCI) fawn pieds are also allowed. All coat colours should be lustrous and clear. Tan, mouse and grey/blue colours are considered highly undesirable in the UK. The American Standard states that solid black (i.e. without a trace of brindle), mouse, liver, black and tan, black and white and white with black are disqualifying faults.

Movement

Despite his muscular build, the French Bulldog's movement should be free and flowing. Viewed from the side, he should use his front and hind legs with equal reach. Absolute soundness should be considered essential.

Size

The French Bulldog's size is evaluated in terms of his weight. The UK Breed Standard stipulates an ideal weight for males of 12.7kg (28lb); females should be 10.9kg (24lb). The American Standard states that dogs must not exceed 12.7kg (28lb), and the FCI Standard gives a weight guide of not below 8kg (17lb) and not over 14kg (30lb).

Summing up

Most Frenchies are kept as pets and will not be seen in the show ring, but breeders should still strive for perfection and attempt to produce dogs that meet the stipulations of the Breed Standard. This is the best way of ensuring that the Frenchie remains sound in mind and body, and retains the characteristics that are unique to this very special breed.

Facing page: A pied dog is predominantly white with coloured patches.

What do you want from your Frenchie?

There are over 200 dog breeds to choose from, so how can you be sure that the French Bulldog is the right breed for you? Before you decide on a Frenchie, you need to be 100 per cent confident that this is the breed that is best suited to your lifestyle.

Companion

Loving and affectionate, the French Bulldog is an ideal companion dog as he wants nothing more than to be with his people. He is easy going and tolerant, and has a degree of adaptability which means that he will adjust to many different lifestyles.

If you have a family with small children, the Frenchie will fit in perfectly. He is not too big and boisterous, but neither is he too small and delicate for the rigours of family life. He needs to be taught to be calm and sensible around children, but he seems to have a natural affinity with them and will enjoy joining in their games. In terms of providing entertainment, he is second to none!

The Frenchie is also a good choice for owners more advanced in years. He thrives on being the centre of attention and will take delight in the most low-key events; he is simply happy to be included in everything that is going on. His exercise needs are moderate. He enjoys a leisurely stroll but he is certainly not built for long and demanding treks.

Sports dog

If you want to get involved in one of the canine sports, a French Bulldog may not be an obvious choice, but don't write him off! This is an intelligent breed, and if you can make training seem like fun, your Frenchie will do his bit!

For more information, see Opportunities for Frenchies page 156.

Show dog

Do you have ambitions to exhibit your French Bulldog in the show ring? This is a highly competitive sport, with big entries in all the classes, so you do need the right dog to begin with.

If you plan to show your Frenchie you need to track down a show quality puppy, and train him so he will perform in the show ring, and accept the detailed 'hands on' examination to which he will be subjected when he is being judged.

It is also important to bear in mind that not every puppy with show potential develops into a top-quality specimen, and so you must be prepared to love your French Bulldog and give him a home for life, even if he doesn't make the grade.

What does your Frenchie want from you?

A dog cannot speak for himself, so we need to view the world from a canine perspective and work out what a French Bulldog needs in order to live a happy, contented and fulfilling life.

Time and commitment

First of all, a French Bulldog needs a commitment that you will care for him for the duration of his life, guiding him through his puppyhood, enjoying his adulthood, and being there for him in his later years.

If all potential owners were prepared to make this pledge, there would be scarcely any dogs in rescue.

The French Bulldog is a superb companion dog, but this comes at a price. He loves to be with his

own special people, and this means that he will be thoroughly miserable if he is excluded from family activities, or expected to spend lengthy periods on his own.

It is important that all dogs can cope with spending some time on their own so they don't become anxious in this situation, but the maximum time a dog should be left is four hours. If this does not fit in with your lifestyle, you should delay owning a dog until your circumstances change.

Practical matters

The French Bulldog is a low maintenance dog when it comes to looking after him. In terms of coat care, his needs are very simple; he is not a great foodie but if you find a diet that suits him, he will do well.

The Frenchie enjoys his exercise, but this is more in terms of exploring new places rather than going on route marches. For the Frenchie, variety is the spice of life.

Leadership

If you choose a small dog, it is sometimes easy to fall into the trap of thinking that leadership and training are not really relevant.

But no dog, even one as charming as a Frenchie, comes instinctively knowing what is right and wrong and effortlessly fitting into your lifestyle.

It is your job to show your Frenchie how you want him to behave by rewarding the behaviour that you consider desirable.

You need to be 100 per cent consistent, so your Frenchie is left in no doubt as to what is deemed acceptable.

If he pushes the boundaries or misbehaves, interrupt his undesirable behaviour by ignoring him if he is attention-seeking (see page 129) or by refocusing his attention if he is refusing to give up something he values (see page 155).

As soon as your Frenchie makes the 'right' decision and changes his behaviour, you can reward him handsomely.

In this way, your Frenchie learns good manners without the need for force or coercion. He is living with you in peace and harmony because he loves and respects you.

Extra Considerations

Now you have decided that a French Bulldog is the dog of your dreams, you can narrow your choice so you know exactly what you are looking for.

Male or female?

The choice of male or female French Bulldog comes down to personal preference. Males are slightly bigger than females, but this is not of major significance. In terms of temperament, there is little to choose between the two sexes – both are equally loving and affectionate. Some say that females are a little more independent minded, but when it comes down to it, Frenchies are all very much individuals.

If you opt for a female, you will need to cope with her seasons, which will start at any time from six to nine months of age and occur approximately every six months thereafter.

During the three-week period of a season, you will need to keep your bitch away from entire males (males that have not been neutered) to eliminate the risk of an unwanted pregnancy. Some owners also report that females may be a little moody and withdrawn during their seasonal cycle.

Many pet owners opt for neutering, which puts an end to the seasons, and also and has many attendant health benefits. The operation, known as spaying, is usually carried out at some point after the first season. The best plan is to seek advice from your vet.

An entire male may not cause many problems, although some do have a stronger tendency to mark, which could include inside the house. However, training will usually put a stop to this. An entire male will also be on the lookout for bitches in season, and this may lead to difficulties, depending on your circumstances.

Neutering (castrating) a male is a relatively simple operation, and there are associated health benefits. Again, you should seek advice from your vet.

Colour

Health and temperament should be top of your list of priorities, but you may well have a preference for a particular colour. Fawn offers the greatest choice as it can range from the palest cream to the darkest red. Dogs may or may not have a black facial mask. Smutty coats, which have too many black hairs, are considered undesirable in the show ring.

Brindle shades also range from pale to dark, with or without white markings. Excessive white markings are discouraged as they are more akin to a Boston Terrier's markings.

Pied dogs are predominately white with coloured patches. In the UK, this is restricted to brindle patches, but in other countries fawn pieds are allowed. Although white should predominate, a reasonable amount of colour is encouraged as there is a strong link between deafness and white dogs (see page 185).

More than one?

Owning a French Bulldog can be addictive and you may want to expand your Frenchie population. However, think carefully before you go ahead. Frenchies are sociable dogs and get along with each other perfectly amicably, unless they become jealous over who is having the lion's share of human attention.

This is a scenario that can arise very easily, particularly if one dog is naturally more pushy. It is therefore your responsibility to ensure that you are even-handed when interacting with your Frenchies.

The best plan is to go for a male and a female as they are most likely to form a bond and will have less of a need to challenge each other.

Obviously one or preferably both dogs will need to be neutered . Take care with initial introductions, and make sure you are very aware of the way the two dogs react to each other, particularly when they are vying for attention from their human family.

Two puppies of the same or similar ages will bond closely with each other.

Be wary of a breeder who encourages you to buy two puppies from the same litter, as it is unlikely that the welfare of the puppies is their top priority.

Most responsible breeders have a waiting list of potential purchasers before a litter is even born and have no need to make this type of sale.

If you do decide to take on a second Frenchie, wait at least 18 months so your first dog is fully trained and settled before embarking on a puppy.

An older dog

You may decide to miss out on the puppy phase and take on an older dog instead. Such a dog may be harder to track down, but sometimes a breeder may have a youngster that is not suitable for showing, but is perfect for a family pet. In some cases, a breeder may rehome a female when her breeding career is at an end so she will enjoy the benefits of more individual attention.

There are advantages to taking on an older dog, as you know exactly what you are getting. But the upheaval of changing homes can be quite upsetting, so you will need to have plenty of patience during the settling in period.

Rehoming a rescued dog

We are fortunate that the number of French Bulldogs that end up in rescue is relatively small. This may be because the breed is not one of the most popular, and may also be because Frenchies are generally easy to live with. However, there are a number of French Bulldogs that need rehoming through no fault of their own. The reasons are various, ranging from illness or death of the original owner to family breakdown, changing jobs, or even the arrival of a new baby.

You are unlikely to find a Frenchie in an all-breed rescue centre; contacting a specialist breed club that runs a rescue scheme will be your best option if you decide to go down this route.

Try to find out as much as you can about a dog's history so you know exactly what you are taking on. You need to be aware of age and health status, likes and dislikes, plus any behavioural issues that may be relevant. You need to be realistic about what you are capable of achieving so you can be sure you can give the dog in question a permanent home.

Regardless of the dog's previous history, you will need to give him plenty of time and be patient with him as he settles into his new home.

It may take weeks, or even months before he becomes fully integrated in the family, but if all goes well you will have the reward of knowing that you have given a Frenchie a second chance.

Sourcing a puppy

Your aim is to find a healthy puppy that is typical of the breed, and has been reared with the greatest possible care. Where do you start?

A tried and trusted method of finding a puppy is to attend a dog show where your chosen breed is being exhibited. This will give you the opportunity to see lots of different French Bulldogs. You will see the different colours, and when you look closely you will detect that there are different 'types' on show. They are all pure-bred Frenchies, but breeders produce dogs with a family likeness, so you can see which type you prefer.

When judging has been completed, talk to the exhibitors and find out more about their dogs. They may not have puppies available, but some will be planning a litter, and you may decide to put your name on a waiting list.

Internet research

The Internet is an excellent resource, but when it comes to finding a puppy, use it with care:

DO go to the website of your national kennel club.

Both the American Kennel Club (AKC) and the Kennel Club (KC) have excellent websites which will give you information about the French Bulldog as a breed, and what to look for when choosing a puppy. You will also find contact details for specialist breed clubs (see below).

Both sites have lists of puppies available, and you can look out for breeders of merit (AKC) and assured breeders (KC) which indicates that a code of conduct has been adhered to.

DO find details of specialist breed clubs.

On breed club websites you will find lots of useful information which will help you to care for your French Bulldog. There may be contact details of breeders in your area, or you may need to go through the club secretary. Some websites also have a list of breeders that have puppies available.

The advantage of going through a breed club is that members will follow a code of ethics, and this will give you some guarantees regarding breeding stock and health checks.

If you are planning to show your French Bulldog you will obviously go to a breeder that has had some success in the ring, so you will need to do additional research to discover more about their breeding lines and the type of French Bulldog they produce.

DO NOT look at puppies for sale.

There are legitimate French Bulldog breeders with their own websites, and they may, occasionally, advertise a litter, although in most cases reputable breeders have waiting lists for their puppies.

The danger comes from unscrupulous breeders that produce puppies purely for profit, with no thought for the health of the dogs they breed from and no care given to rearing the litter.

Photos of puppies are hard to resist, but never make a decision based purely on an advertisement. You need to find out who the breeder is, and have the opportunity to visit their premises and inspect the litter before making a decision.

Questions, questions, questions

- When you find a breeder with puppies available, you will have lots of questions to ask. These should include the following:

- Where have the puppies been reared? Hopefully,

they will be in a home environment which gives them the best possible start in life.

- How many are in the litter?
- What is the split of males and females?
- What colours are available?
- How many have already been spoken for? The breeder will probably be keeping a puppy to show or for breeding, and there may be others on a waiting list.
- Can I see the mother with her puppies?
- What age are the puppies?
- When will they be ready to go to their new homes?

Bear in mind puppies need to be with their mother and siblings until they are eight weeks of age otherwise they miss out on vital learning and communication skills, which will have a detrimental effect on them for the rest of their lives.

You should also be prepared to answer a number of searching questions so the breeder can check if you are suitable as a potential owner of one of their precious puppies.

You will be asked some or all of the following questions:

- What is your home set up?
- Do you have children/grandchildren?
- What are their ages?
- Do you have a securely-fenced garden?
- Is there somebody at home the majority of the time?
- What is your previous experience with dogs?
- Do you already have other dogs at home?
- Do you have plans to show your French Bulldog?

It is important to see the mother with her puppies.

The breeder is not being intrusive; he needs to understand the type of home you will be able to provide in order to make the right match. Do not be offended by this; the breeder is doing it both for your, and the dog's, benefit.

Steer clear of a breeder who does not ask you questions. He or she may be more interested in making money out of the puppies than ensuring that they go to good homes.

They may also have taken other shortcuts which may prove disastrous, and very expensive, in terms of vet bills or plain heartache.

Health issues

In common with all pure-bred dogs, the French Bulldog suffers from some hereditary problems so you need to talk to the breeder about the health status of breeding stock and find out if there are any issues of concern.

For information on inherited conditions and breed specific conditions, see page 182.

Facing page: The breeder needs to be sure that you can provide a home that suits the needs of a French Bulldog.

Puppy watching

French Bulldogs puppies are totally irresistible. Looking like adults in miniature, they are brimming with personality, and each puppy seems to be saying: 'pick me!' However, you must not to let your heart rule your head.

Try to put your feelings to one side so that you can make an informed choice.

You need to be 100 per cent confident that the breeding stock is healthy, and the puppies have been reared with love and care, before making a commitment to buy.

Viewing a litter

It is a good idea to have mental checklist of what to look out for when you visit a breeder. You want to see:

- A clean, hygienic environment.
- Puppies who are out-going, friendly, and eager to meet you.
- A sweet-natured mother who is ready to show off her pups.
- Puppies that are well covered, but not pot-bellied, which could be an indication of worms.
- Bright eyes, with no sign of soreness or discharge.
- Clean ears that smell fresh.
- No discharge from the ears or the nose.
- Clean rear ends – matting could indicate an upset tummy.

It is important that you see the mother with her

puppies as this will give you a good idea of the temperament they are likely to inherit. It is also helpful if you can see other close relatives so you can see the type of French Bulldog the breeder produces.

In most cases, you will not be able to see the father (sire) as most breeders will travel some distance to find a stud dog that is not too close to their own bloodlines and complements their bitch. However, you should be able to see photos of him and be given the chance to examine his pedigree and show record.

Companion puppy

If you are looking for a Frenchie as a companion, you should be guided by the breeder who will have spent hours and hours puppy watching, and will know each of the pups as an individual. It is tempting to choose a puppy yourself, but the breeder will take into account your family set up and lifestyle and will help you to pick the most suitable puppy.

Show puppy

If you are buying a puppy with the hope of showing him, make sure you make this clear to the breeder.

A lot of planning goes into producing a litter, and although all the puppies will have been reared with equal care, there will be one or two that have show potential. Ideally, recruit a breed expert to inspect the puppies with you so you have the benefit of their objective evaluation. The breeder will also be there to help as they will want to ensure that only the best of their stock is exhibited in the show ring. Wait until the puppies are between seven and eight weeks before making your choice as this gives them time to develop.

By the time the puppies are six weeks of age, their ears should be erect. French Bulldog puppies are born with their ears down, and they start to go up from four weeks onwards, though they can be up one minute and down the next for a few weeks! Teething, which occurs at around four months, will also affect ear carriage.

The head should be fairly large and wide, with a broad muzzle.

The correct jaw is important in the breed; by eight weeks a puppy should have a reverse scissor bite where the teeth on the lower jaw close over the teeth on the upper jaw.

French Bulldogs are born with a short tail, and sometimes no tail at all. This occurs naturally; tails are never docked. Sometimes the tail will stick straight out in a young puppy, but this generally settles as the dog matures and lies flat, but not tightly clamped, over the anus. A tail that sticks straight up is likely to stay that way, and, although this is fine for a pet, it would not be acceptable in the show ring.

A puppy will go through many stages as he is growing up - the most beautiful puppy can grow through an ugly duckling phase. However if the basic conformation is correct, there is a good chance that your pup will mature into a sound, typical representative of the breed. Whether he has the star quality that will make him a winner in the show ring is purely a matter of luck...

A Frenchie-friendly home

It may seem an age before your French Bulldog puppy is ready to leave the breeder and move to his new home. But you can fill the time by getting your home ready, and buying the equipment you will need. These preparations apply to a new puppy but, in reality, they are the means of creating an environment that is safe and secure for your Frenchie throughout his life.

In the home

Nothing is safe when a puppy is about, and that is certainly true if you have a Frenchie in the house! It is all new and exciting for a young puppy, and he

They never
Vary!

will investigate everything with his mouth, which can lead him into all sorts of mischief. One thing is certain; a free-ranging French Bulldog puppy cannot be trusted.

Remember, it is not only your prized possessions that are under threat – the damage a puppy can inflict on himself is equally relevant.

Trailing electric cables are a major hazard so these will need to be secured out of reach. You will need to make sure all cupboards and storage units cannot be opened or broken into.

This applies particularly in the kitchen where you may store cleaning materials, and other substances which could be toxic to dogs. There are a number of household plants that are poisonous, so these will need to relocated, along with breakable ornaments.

You may decide to declare upstairs off-limits and this is a sensible decision, particularly as negotiating stairs can be hazardous for a young puppy.

The best way of doing this is to install a baby gate; these can also be useful if you want to limit your French Bulldog's freedom in any other part of the house. This barrier works well as your dog is separate but does not feel excluded from what is going on.

In the garden

A French Bulldog does not have a great desire to roam but curiosity can get the better of him, and he may find his way out of hedging or insubstantial fencing. Before your puppy arrives home make sure that your garden is securely fenced, and also check that gates leading out of your property have secure fastenings.

Do not underestimate a Frenchie's desire to explore.

There are a number of plants that are toxic to dogs, such as tulip bulbs, lily of the valley, azaleas, jasmine and daffodil flowers. You can find a comprehensive list on the internet. Remove the offending plants, or limit access to them before your puppy comes home.

You also need to be aware that garden chemicals, such as fertilisers, fungicides and pesticides, are highly toxic so be very careful where you use them.

Swimming pools and ponds should be covered, as most puppies are fearless and, although it is easy for a puppy to take the plunge, it is virtually impossible for him to get out, potentially with lethal consequences. You will also need to designate a toileting area. This will assist the house training process, and it will also make cleaning up easier. For information on house-training, see page 96.

House rules

Before your puppy comes home, hold a family conference to make the house rules. You need to decide which rooms your puppy will have access to, and establish whether he is to be allowed on the furniture or not. It is important to start as you mean to go on. You cannot invite a puppy on to the sofa for cuddles only to decide in a few months' time that this is no longer desirable.

The French Bulldog likes to please, but he will push it if he doesn't know where his boundaries lie. If house rules are applied consistently, he will understand what is, and what is not, allowed, and he will learn to respect you and co-operate with you.

Buying equipment

There are some essential items of equipment you will need for your French Bulldog. If you choose wisely, much of it will last for many years to come.

Indoor crate

Rearing a puppy is so much easier if you invest in an indoor crate. It provides a safe haven for your puppy at night, when you have to go out during the day, and at other times when you cannot supervise him. A puppy needs a base where he feels safe and secure, and where he can rest undisturbed. An indoor crate provides the perfect den, and many adults continue to use them throughout their lives.

You will also need to consider where you are going to locate the crate. The kitchen is usually the most suitable place as this is the hub of family life. Try to find a snug corner where the puppy can rest when he wants to, but where he can also see what is going on around him, and still be with the family.

Beds and bedding

The crate will need to be lined with bedding and the best type to buy is synthetic fleece. This is warm and cosy, and as moisture soaks through it, your puppy will not have a wet bed when he is tiny and is still unable to go through the night without relieving himself. This type of bedding is machine washable and easy to dry; buy two pieces, so you have one to use while the other piece is in the wash.

If you have purchased a crate, you may not feel the need to buy an extra bed, although your Frenchie may like to have a bed in the family room so he feels part of household activities. There is an amazing array of dog-beds to chose from – duvets, bean bags, cushions, baskets, igloos, mini-four posters – so you can take your pick! However, you do need to bear in mind that a puppy may enjoy chewing his bed, so it may be worth delaying this purchase until your Frenchie is beyond the teething phase.

Collar and lead

You may think that it is not worth buying a collar for the first few weeks, but the sooner your pup gets used to it, the better (see Wearing a Collar, page 138). A nylon lightweight collar is recommended as most puppies will accept it without making a fuss. Be careful when you are fitting the collar that is not too

Your home is a place where your Frenchie should feel safe and secure.

tight, but equally not too loose as slipping the collar can become a favourite game...

A thin, matching webbing lead will be fine to begin with; the last thing you want is for your puppy to feel weighed down by a heavy collar and lead. An extending lead can be a useful purchase as you can give your Frenchie limited freedom when it is not safe or permitted to allow him off lead. However, you should never use it when walking alongside roads as an unexpected pull from your Frenchie resulting in the lead extending further than you want, could have disastrous consequences.

ID

Your French Bulldog needs to wear some form of ID when he is out in public places. This can be in the form of a disc, engraved with your contact details, attached to the collar. When your Frenchie is full-grown, you can buy an embroidered collar with your contact details, which eliminates the danger of the disc becoming detached from the collar.

You may also wish to consider a permanent form of ID. Increasingly breeders are getting puppies microchipped before they go to their new homes. A microchip is the size of a grain of rice. It is injected under the skin, usually between the shoulder blades, with a special needle. It has tiny barbs on it, which dig into the tissue around where it lies, so it does not migrate from that spot.

Each chip has its own unique identification number which can only be read by a special scanner. That ID number is then registered on a national database with your name and details, so that if ever your dog is lost, he can be taken to any vet or rescue centre where he is scanned and then you are contacted. If your puppy has not been microchipped, you can ask your vet to do it, maybe when he goes for his vaccinations.

Bowls

Your French Bulldog will need two bowls; one for food, and one for fresh drinking water, which should always be readily available. A stainless steel bowl is a good choice for a food as it is tough and hygienic. Plastic bowls will almost certainly be chewed, and there is a danger that bacteria can collect in the small cracks that may appear.

You can opt for a second stainless steel bowl for drinking water, or you may prefer a heavier ceramic bowl which will not be knocked over so easily.

Food

The breeder will let you know what your puppy is eating and should provide a full diet sheet to guide you through the first six months of your puppy's feeding regime – how much they are eating per meal, how many meals per day, when to increase the amounts given per meal and when to reduce the meals per day.

The breeder may provide you with some food when you go and collect your puppy, but it is worth making enquiries in advance about the availability of the brand that is recommended.

Toys

French Bulldogs puppies love to play, and there is no shortage of dog toys on the market. But before you get carried away with buying a vast range of toys to keep your puppy entertained, think about possible hazards.

A puppy can easily chew bits from soft or plastic toys, and if this material is ingested it can cause serious problems in the form of a blockage.

The safest toys to choose are made of hard rubber; a rubber kong which can be stuffed with food is ideal. You can also buy rope tug toys, but be careful how you play with your dog, particularly while he is teething. Frenchies also like to play with balls. Again, go for a rubber ball and make sure it is big enough so it cannot be swallowed.

Frenchies, young and old, love to play...

Grooming gear

The French Bulldog is a fairly low maintenance breed in terms of coat but there are a few bare essentials you will need:

- Soft brush to use while your puppy is becoming accustomed to grooming.
- Hound glove/rubber brush for adult coat care.
- Nail-clippers – the guillotine type are easy to use.
- Toothbrush and toothpaste: Choose between a long-handled toothbrush or a finger brush – whichever you find easiest to use. There are flavoured canine toothpastes on the market which are acceptable to your dog.
- Cotton-wool (cotton) for cleaning the eyes, ears and facial wrinkles.
- Petroleum jelly to apply after cleaning the wrinkles.

Finding a vet

Before your puppy arrives home, you should register with a vet. Visit several vets in your local area, or speak to other pet owners that you might know, to see who they recommend.

It is so important to find a good vet – almost as much as finding a good doctor for yourself. You need to find someone with whom you can build up a good rapport and have complete faith in. Word of mouth is really the best recommendation.

When you contact a veterinary practice, find out the following:

- Does the surgery run an appointment system?
- What are the arrangements for emergency, out of hours cover?
- Do any of the vets in the practice have experience treating French Bulldogs?
- What facilities are available at the practice?

If you are satisfied with what your find, and the staff appear to be helpful and friendly, book an appointment so your puppy can have a health check a couple of days after you collect him.

Settling in

When you first arrive home with your puppy, be careful not to overwhelm him. You and your family are hugely excited, but the puppy is in a completely strange environment with new sounds, smells and sights, which is a daunting experience, even for the boldest of pups.

Some puppies are very confident, wanting to play straightaway and quickly making friends; others need a little longer. Keep a close check on your puppy's body language and reactions so you can proceed at a pace he is comfortable with.

First, let him explore the garden. He will probably need to relieve himself after the journey home, so take him to the allocated toileting area and, when he performs, give him plenty of praise.

When you take your puppy indoors, let him investigate again. Show him his crate, and encourage him to go in by throwing in a treat.

Let him have a sniff, and allow him to go in and out as he wants to. Later on, when he is tired, you can put him in the crate while you stay in the room. In this way he will learn to settle and will not think he is being abandoned.

It is a good idea to feed your puppy in his crate, at least to begin with, as this helps to build up a positive association. It will not be long before your Frenchie sees his crate as his own special den and will go there as a matter of choice. Some owners place a blanket over the crate, covering the back and sides, so that it is even more cosy and den-like.

Meeting the family

Resist the temptation of inviting friends and neighbours to come and meet the new arrival; your puppy needs to focus on getting to know his new family for the first few days. Try not to swamp your Frenchie with too much attention; give him a chance to explore and find his feet. There will be plenty of time for cuddles later on!

If you have children in the family, you need to keep everything as calm as possible. Your puppy may not have met children before, and even if he has, he will still find them strange and unpredictable. A puppy can become alarmed by too much noise, or he may go to the opposite extreme and become over-excited, which can lead to mouthing and nipping. The best plan is to get the children to sit on the floor and give them all a treat. Each child can then call the puppy, stroke him, and offer a treat. In this way the puppy is making the decisions rather than being forced into interactions he may find stressful.

If he tries to nip or mouth, make sure there is a toy at the ready, so his attention can be diverted to something he is allowed to bite. If you do this consistently, he will learn to inhibit his desire to mouth when he is interacting with people.

Right from the start, impose a rule that the children are not allowed to pick up or carry the puppy. They can cuddle him when they are sitting on the floor. This may sound a little severe, but a wriggly puppy can be dropped in an instant, sometimes with disastrous consequences.

If possible, try to make sure your Frenchie is only given attention when he has all four feet on the ground. This is a breed than can be attention seeking so if your pup learns that jumping up and demanding attention is not rewarding, it will pay dividends later on.

Involve all family members with the day-to-day care of your puppy; this will enable the bond to develop with the whole family as opposed to just one person. Encourage the children to train and reward the puppy, teaching him to follow their commands without question.

The animal family

Great care must be taken when introducing a puppy to a resident dog to ensure that relations get off on the right footing. Frenchies do have a jealous streak so you need to ensure that you are even handed in all your dealings. If the two dogs are confident of their place in your affections, they will not need to vie with each other for attention.

Your adult dog may be allowed to meet the puppy at the breeder's, which is ideal as the older dog will not feel threatened if he is away from home. But if this is not possible, allow your dog to smell the puppy's bedding (the bedding supplied by the breeder is fine) before they actually meet so he familiarizes himself with the puppy's scent.

The garden is the best place for introducing the puppy, as the adult will regard it as neutral territory. He will probably take a great interest in the puppy and sniff him all over. Most puppies are naturally submissive in this situation, and your pup may lick the other dog's mouth or roll over on to his back. Try not to interfere as this is the natural way that dogs get to know each other. You will only need to intervene if the older dog is too boisterous, and alarms the puppy. In this case, it is a good idea to put the adult on his lead so you have some measure of control.

It rarely takes long for an adult to accept a puppy, as he does not constitute a threat. This will be underlined if you make a big fuss of the older dog so that he has no reason to feel jealous. But no matter how well the two dogs are getting on, do not leave them alone unless one is crated.

Below: Frenchies are sociable and enjoy the company of other dogs.

If early interactions are supervised, a Frenchie will live in harmony with the family cat.

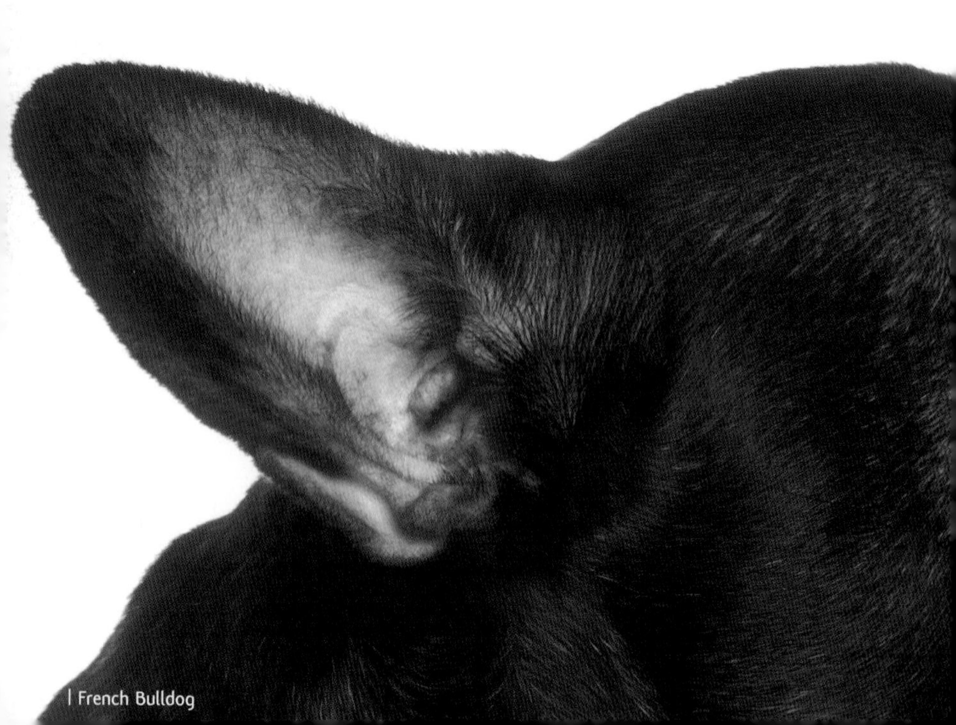

Feline friends

The French Bulldog is a tolerant animal and he will learn to live peaceably with the family cat. There will always be the odd occasion when he can't resist a chase 'just for fun', but most of the time cat and dog will co-exist peacefully.

However, it is important to supervise early interactions so you establish the ground rules. Bear in mind that a Frenchie has large, fairly prominent eyes, and one swipe from a cat's claw could cause a lot of damage. It may be easier if the cat is confined in a carrier for the first couple of meetings so your puppy has a chance to make his acquaintance in a controlled situation.

Keep calling your puppy to you and rewarding him so that he does not focus too intently on the cat. You can then graduate to holding your puppy while the cat is free, again rewarding him with a treat every time he responds to you and looks away from the cat. When you allow your puppy to go free, make sure the cat has an easy escape route, just in case he tries to chase.

This is an on-going process but, all the time your Frenchie is learning that he is rewarded for ignoring the cat. In time, the novelty will wear off and the pair will mostly ignore each other. In some cases, a

Frenchie and the family cat will become the best of friends and end up sharing a bed!

Feeding

The breeder will generally provide enough food for the first few days so the puppy does not have to cope with a change in diet – and possible digestive upset – along with all the stress of moving home.

Some puppies eat up their food from the first meal onwards, others are more concerned by their new surroundings and are too distracted to eat. French Bulldogs are not obsessed by food like some dogs, such as Labradors, but they will generally eat their rations with moderate enthusiasm. Therefore, there is no need to worry if your puppy seems disinterested in his food for the first day or so. Give him 10 minutes to eat what he wants and then remove the leftovers and start afresh at the next meal. Obviously if you have any concerns about your puppy in the first few days, seek advice from your vet.

French Bulldogs can sometimes become possessive, and this behaviour can be seen at mealtimes if a Frenchie is insecure and feels the need to guard his food bowl. It is therefore important that you give your dog a space where he can eat in peace, and if you have children, you need to establish a rule that no one is to go near the dog when he is feeding. This is sound commonsense, and removes all risk of problems arising, no matter how unintentional they may be.

However, there is plenty of scope for you to work on your Frenchie's manners so that he does not feel protective of his food bowl. You can do this by giving him half his ration, and then dropping food around his bowl. This will stop him guarding his bowl and, at the same time, he will see your presence in a positive light. You can also call him away from the bowl and reward him with food – maybe something extra special – which he can take from your hand.

Start doing this as soon as your puppy arrives in his new home, and continue working on it throughout his life.

The first night

Your puppy will have spent the first weeks of his life with either his mother or curled up with his siblings. He is then taken from everything he knows as familiar, lavished with attention by his new family, and then comes bed time when he is left all alone. It is little wonder that he feels abandoned.

The best plan is to establish a nighttime routine, and then stick to it so that your puppy knows what is expected of him. Take your puppy out into the garden to relieve himself, and then settle him in his crate. Some people leave a low light on for the puppy at night for the first week, others have tried a radio as company or a ticking clock. A covered hot-water bottle, filled with warm water, can also be a comfort. Like people, puppies are all individuals and what works for one, does not necessarily work for another, so it is a matter of trial and error.

Be very positive when you leave your puppy on his own; do not linger, or keep returning; this will make the situation more difficult. It is

Your puppy will soon learn he is not being abandoned when you leave him at night.

inevitable that he will protest to begin with, but if you stick to your routine, he will accept that he gets left at night but you always return in the morning.

Rescued dogs

Settling an older, rescued dog in the home is very similar to a puppy in as much as you will need to make the same preparations regarding his homecoming. As with a puppy, an older dog will need you to be consistent, so start as you mean to go on.

There is often an initial honeymoon period when you bring a rescued dog home, where he will be on his best behaviour for the first few weeks. It is after these first couple of weeks that the true nature of the dog will show, so be prepared for subtle changes in his behaviour.

It may be advisable to register with a reputable training club, so you can seek advice on any training or behavioural issues at an early stage.

Above all, remember that a rescued dog ceases to be a rescued dog the moment he enters his forever home and should be treated normally like any other family pet.

A rescued dog make take some time to settle.

House training

This is an aspect of training that first-time owners dread, but if you start as you mean to go on, it will not be long before your French Bulldog understands what is required.

The key to successful house training is vigilance and consistency. If you establish a routine, and you stick to it, your puppy will understand what is required.

Equally, you must be there to supervise him at all times, except when he is safely tucked up in his crate. It is when a puppy is left to wander from room that accidents happen.

As discussed earlier, you will have allocated a toileting area in your garden when preparing for your puppy's homecoming. You need to take your puppy to this area every time he needs to relieve himself so he builds up an association and knows why you have

brought him out to the garden.

Establish a routine and make sure you take your puppy out at the following times:

- First thing in the morning
- After mealtimes
- On waking
- Following a play session
- Last thing at night.

A puppy should be taken out to relieve himself every two hours as an absolute minimum. If you can manage an hourly trip out, so much the better. The more often your puppy gets it right, the quicker he will learn to be clean in the house. It helps if you use a verbal cue, such as 'Busy', when your pup is performing and, in time, this will trigger the desired response.

Do not be tempted to put your puppy out on the doorstep in the hope that he will toilet on his own. Most pups simply sit there, waiting to get back inside the house! No matter how bad the weather is, accompany your puppy and give him lots of praise when he performs correctly.

Do not rush back inside as soon as he has finished; your puppy might start to delay in the hope of prolonging his time outside with you. Praise him, have a quick game, and then you can both return indoors.

When accidents happen

No matter how vigilant you are, there are bound to be accidents. If you witness the accident, take your puppy outside immediately, and give him lots of praise if he finishes his business out there.

If you are not there when he has an accident, do not scold him when you discover what has happened. He will not remember what he has done and will not understand why you are cross with him. Simply clean it up and resolve to be more vigilant next time.

Make sure you use a deodoriser, available in pet stores, when you clean up otherwise your pup will be drawn to the smell and may be tempted to use the same spot again.

Choosing a diet

There are so many different types of dog food on sale, all claiming to be the best, so how do you know what is likely to suit your French Bulldog?

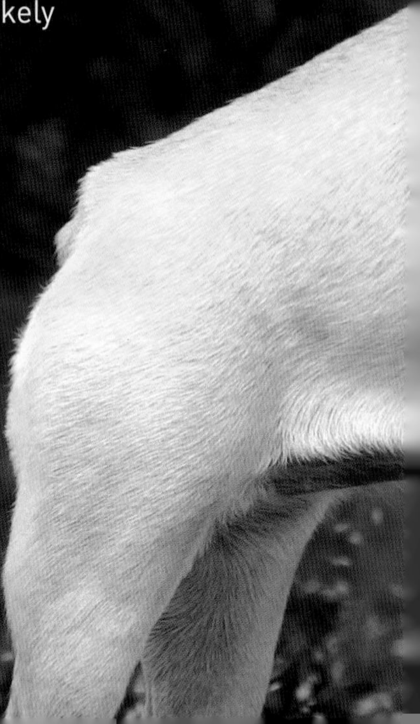

When choosing a diet, there are basically three categories to choose from:

Complete

This is probably the most popular diet as it is easy to feed and is specially formulated with all the nutrients your dog needs. This means that you should not add any supplements or you may upset the nutritional balance.

Most complete diets come in different life stages- puppy, adult maintenance and senior, so this means that your Frenchie is getting what he needs when he is growing, during adulthood, and as he becomes older. You can even get prescription diets for dogs with particular health issues.

Generally, an adult maintenance diet should contain 21 to 24 per cent protein and 10 to 14 per cent fat. Protein levels should be higher in puppy diets, and reduced in veteran diets.

There are many different brands to choose from so it is advisable to seek advice from your puppy's breeder who will have lengthy experience of feeding French Bulldogs.

Some French Bulldogs have a problem with flatulence and this seems to be linked to dogs that are fed a completely dry diet. It is possibly the result of a sluggish digestive system. If this is the case with your Frenchie, you would be advised to change diets (see Barf diets, below).

Canned/pouches

This type of food is usually fed with hard biscuit, and most French Bulldogs find it very appetising. However, the ingredients and the nutritional value do vary significantly between the different brands so you will need to check the label.

This type of food often has a high moisture content, so you need to be sure your Frenchie is getting all the nutrition he needs.

Homemade

There are some owners who like to prepare meals especially for their dogs – and it is probably much appreciated. The danger is that although the food is tasty, and your French Bulldog may appreciate the variety, you cannot be sure that it has the correct nutritional balance.

If this is a route you want to go down, you will need to find out the exact ratio of fats, carbohydrates, proteins, minerals and vitamins that are needed, which is quite an undertaking.

The Barf (Biologically Appropriate Raw Food) diet is another, more natural approach to feeding. Dogs are fed a diet mimicking what they would have eaten in the wild, consisting of raw meat, bone, muscle, fat, and vegetable matter. French Bulldogs do well on this diet, and it seems particularly suitable for dogs that suffer from flatulence.

There are now a number of companies that specialise in producing the Barf diet in frozen form, which will make your job a lot easier.

Feeding regime

When your puppy arrives in his new home he will need four meals, evenly spaced throughout the day. You may decide to keep to the diet recommended by your puppy's breeder, and if your pup is thriving there is no need to change.

However, if your puppy is not doing well on the food, or you have problems with supply, you will need to make a change. When switching diets, it is very important to do it on a gradual basis, changing over from one food to the next, a little at a time, and spreading the transition over a week to 10 days. This will avoid the risk of digestive upset. Breeds vary in the length of time they take to reach full maturity; French Bulldogs should be considered full adults at around two years of age.

The breeder will give advice on diet based on extensive experience.

As discussed, puppies need a higher ratio of protein than adult dogs, and dogs aged from 9-18 months will need a larger quantity of food than a mature adult. Rations should be spread over three meals a day, decreasing to two meals of an adult maintenance diet when the dog is fully mature.

Faddy feeders

As already observed, the French Bulldog is not passionate about his food and so there is the very real danger that you may start trying to tempt his appetite.

One look from those gorgeous dark eyes is enough to melt your heart, stirring you to greater efforts to find a food that your Frenchie will really like.

At first you may add some gravy, then you may try some chicken... The Frenchie is far from stupid, and he will quickly realise that if he holds out, tastier treats will follow.

This is a bad game to play as not only will you run out of tempting delicacies, you will also be losing your Frenchie's respect.

If your Frenchie is turning up his nose at mealtimes, give him 10 minutes to eat what he wants, and then take up his bowl.

Do not feed him treats in between meals, and give him fresh food at his next mealtime. If you continue this regime for a couple of days, your Frenchie will realize that there is no percentage in holding out for better food as it never materialises.

In most cases, this is just a 'trying it on' phase, and if you cope with commonsense, you will soon return to the status quo and your Frenchie will be content with his normal rations.

If, however, your dog refuses all food for more than 24 hours you need to observe his behaviour to see if there are any signs of ill health, which may involve the need for a veterinary check up.

Regurgitation

Some French Bulldogs may regurgitate their food, undigested, immediately after eating. Others may gulp down water and then regurgitate. If this happens on an occasional basis, there is no cause for concern, but if it occurs regularly it needs to be investigated.

There is a risk that regular regurgitation signals a serious condition which will need veterinary exploration.

However, with French Bulldogs there may be other causes which you can address. In many cases, it is a reaction to a certain type of food, such as a dry pellet diet (often with a high grain content), and a switch to a more natural Barf diet (see page 103) may solve the problem.

As well as a change of diet, you can try feeding three

smaller meals per day. Adding a spoonful of plain yoghurt and feeding from a raised bowl about 7.5cm (3in) from the floor can also be effective.

The golden rule is not to feed your Frenchie when he is excited, when he has just drunk a lot of water, and not before or after exercise. In all cases, make sure your Frenchie is allowed to rest quietly after he has eaten his meal.

Bones and chews

Puppies love to chew, and many adults also enjoy gnawing on a bone. A raw marrow bone is ideal, but make sure it is always given under supervision.

Nylon bones are also a favourite with Frenchies. They come in a variety of sizes and flavours, and some have raised nodules which are excellent for keeping teeth clean. Rawhide chews are best avoided; it is all too easy for a Frenchie to bite off a chunk and swallow it, with the danger of it then causing a blockage.

Ideal weight

In order to help to keep your French Bulldog in good health it is necessary to monitor his weight. As a breed, Frenchies are not prone to obesity as they are not greedy dogs, but there are always exceptions to the rule.

A dog that is carrying too much weight is vulnerable to many health issues; he has a reduced quality of life as he cannot exercise properly, and he will almost certainly have a reduced life expectancy.

When judging a French Bulldog's condition, look at him from above, and make sure you can see a definite waist. You should be able to feel his ribs, but not see them.

If you are concerned about your Frenchie's weight, get into the habit of visiting your veterinary surgery on a monthly basis so that you can weigh him. You can keep a record of his weight so you can make adjustments if necessary.

If you are concerned that your Frenchie is putting on too much weight, or equally if you think he is underweight, consult your vet who will help you to plan a suitable diet.

Facing page: If you keep your Frenchie at the correct weight he will be able to enjoy life to the full.

Caring for your French Bulldog

The French Bulldog is classed as a low maintenance breed, but like all animals, a Frenchie has his own special needs which you must take on board.

Coat care

With his short coat, a French Bulldog needs minimal grooming – and a puppy requires even less – but do not make the mistake of ignoring this aspect of his care. A grooming session gives you the opportunity to check your dog and to discover any minor problems, such as sore places, or any abnormalities, such as lumps and bumps, which may need to be investigated. Remember, if you spot a problem early on, you increase the chance of an early diagnosis and successful treatment.

The first step is to get your puppy used to being handled so that he accepts the attention without resentment. Initially, he will wriggle and attempt to mouth you, but just ignore his protests. Hold him steady for a few moments, and reward him when he is still. A puppy needs to learn that it is OK to be touched all over; if you fail to do this, he may try to warn you off by growling, which could develop into more problematic behaviour.

Start by handling your puppy all over, stroking him from his head to his tail. Lift up each paw in turn, and reward him with a treat when he co-operates. Then roll him over on to his back and tickle his tummy; this is a very vulnerable position for a dog to adopt, so do not force the issue. Be firm but gentle, and give

Reward your puppy for standing quietly on the grooming table.

The ears can be a sensitive area so be gentle when you examine them.

Pick up each paw in turn.

your Frenchie lots of praise when he does as you ask. When your Frenchie is happy to be handled in this way, you can introduce a soft brush and spend a few minutes working on his coat, and then reward him. He will gradually learn to accept the attention, and will relax while you groom him.

When the adult coat comes through it will be short and smooth with a fine texture. A French Bulldog speciality is the lustrous sheen on a well-groomed, healthy dog. There is no undercoat.

To keep the coat in good order, a quick brush on daily basis is all that is required. A rubber brush or a hound brush work best as they remove both dirt and dead hair from the coat. If you want your Frenchie to look really smart, or if you are taking him into the show ring, a rub down with a chamois leather will bring out the sheen in his coat.

Bathing

A French Bulldog should not be bathed too frequently as it has an adverse effect on the skin's natural oils. Not only does this result in a dull coat, it can also cause a dry, itchy skin. Most owners reckon that every 8 to 12 weeks is sufficient unless the dog has found something particularly revolting to roll in!

Make sure you use a mild moisturising shampoo specially formulated for dogs, and you can also use a conditioner which will improve the quality and appearance of the coat.

It is a good idea to plan your first bath while your Frenchie is still small enough to handle easily. He will then become accustomed to the procedure and bath times will not become a battlefield.

Routine care

In addition to grooming, you will need to carry out some routine care.

Eyes

Check the eyes for signs of soreness or discharge. You can use a piece of cotton wool (cotton) –a separate piece for each eye – and wipe away any debris.

Ears

The ears should be clean and free from odour. You can buy specially manufactured ear wipes, or you can use a piece of cotton wool to clean them if necessary. Do not probe into the ear canal or you risk doing more harm than good.

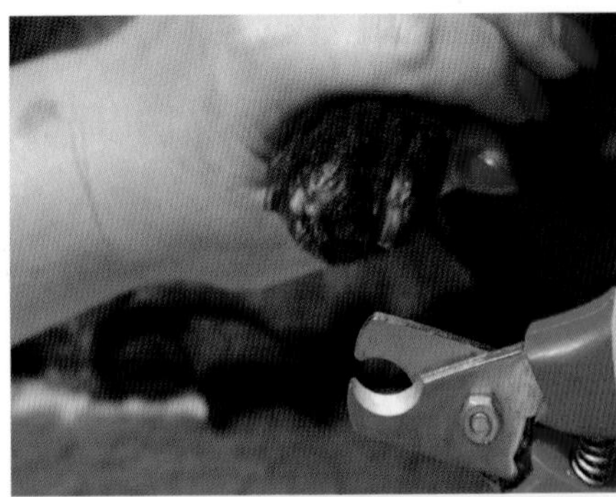

Start nail trimming from an early age.

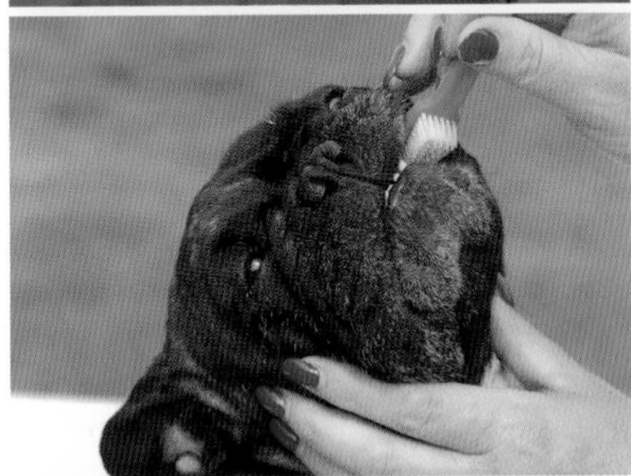

Regular teeth cleaning will prevent tooth decay and gum infection.

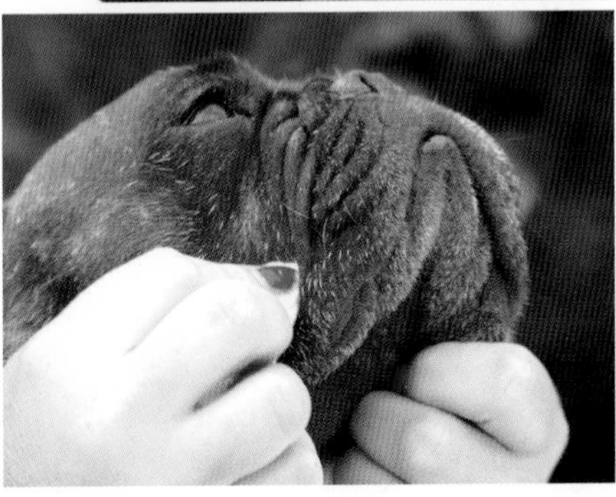

It is essential to keep facial wrinkles clean.

Teeth

Dental disease is becoming more prevalent among dogs so teeth cleaning should be seen as an essential part of your care regime. The build up of tartar on the teeth can result in tooth decay, gum infection and bad breath, and if it is allowed to accumulate, you may have no option but to get the teeth cleaned under anaesthetic.

When your French Bulldog is still a puppy, accustom him to teeth cleaning so it becomes a matter of routine.

Dog toothpaste comes in a variety of meaty flavours, which your Frenchie will like, so you can start by putting some toothpaste on your finger and gently rubbing his teeth. You can then progress to using a finger brush or a toothbrush, whichever you find most convenient.

Remember to reward your Frenchie when he co-operates and then he will positively look forward to his teeth-cleaning sessions.

Nails

Nail trimming is a task dreaded by many owners, and many dogs, but if you start early on, your French Bulldog will get used to the task you have to perform and will not fight against it.

If your dog has white nails, you will be able to see the quick (the vein that runs through the nail), which you must avoid at all costs. If you cut the quick it will bleed profusely and cause considerable discomfort. Obviously, the task is much harder in dark nails as you cannot see the quick. The best policy is to trim little and often so the nails don't grow too long, and you do not risk cutting too much and catching the quick.

If you are worried about trimming your French Bulldog's nails, go to your vet so you can see it done properly. If you are still concerned, you can always use the services of a professional groomer.

Wrinkles

It is absolutely essential that you wipe your Frenchie's facial wrinkles every day. If this task is neglected, infection can build up in the crevices and sores will develop. Not only are these very unsightly, it will cause your dog much pain and discomfort.

To clean the wrinkles, take a wad of cotton wool (cotton), soaked in lukewarm water, or alternatively you can use an unscented wet wipe. Gently wipe along the length of the wrinkle and then dry with cotton-wool or a soft towel. You can then apply a little cream or petroleum jelly.

Exercise

The French Bulldog thrives on having a busy, interesting life, but he does not need a great deal of exercise. It is important that he is kept fit and active, and he will enjoy the opportunity to use his nose and go to different places, but he will generally take things at an easy pace, with an occasional burst of speed for good measure.

As a brachycephalic breed, the French Bulldog's respiratory system is not as efficient as it is in other breeds with a more conventional head structure. This means that a Frenchie can overheat very easily, and he can quickly become distressed. For this reason, you should never exercise your Frenchie in hot weather, and if you are playing a game such as retrieve, stop the game before his breathing becomes laboured.

Digestive problems can be linked with exercise, so make sure you leave at least one hour before and after feeding before you take your Frenchie out.

The older Frenchie

We are fortunate that the French has a pretty good life expectancy – generally around 12 years, and many do slightly better.

As your Frenchie grows older, he may sleep more

and he may be reluctant to go for longer walks. He may show signs of stiffness when he gets up from his bed, but these generally ease when he starts moving. Some older French Bulldogs may have impaired vision, and some may become a little deaf, but as long as their senses do not deteriorate dramatically, this is something older dogs learn to live with.

If you treat your older dog with kindness and consideration, he will enjoy his later years and suffer the minimum of discomfort.

It is advisable to switch him over to a senior diet, which is more suited to his needs, and you may need to adjust the quantity, as he will not be burning up the calories as he did when he was younger and more energetic.

The older Frenchie will often prefer a softer diet, and you will need to keep a close check on his teeth as these may cause problems. Make sure his sleeping quarters are warm and free from draughts, and if he gets wet, make sure you dry him thoroughly.

Most important of all, be guided by your French Bulldog. He will have good days when he feels up to going for a walk, and other days when he would prefer to potter in the garden.

Letting Go

Inevitably there comes a time when your French Bulldog is not enjoying a good quality of life, and you need to make the painful decision to let him go. We would all wish that our dogs died, painlessly, in their sleep but, unfortunately, this is rarely the case.

However, we can allow our dogs to die with dignity, and to suffer as a little as possible, and this should be our way of saying thank you for the wonderful companionship they have given us.

When you feel the time is drawing close, talk to your vet who will be able to make an objective assessment of your French Bulldog's condition and will help you to make the right decision.

This is the hardest thing you will ever have to do as a dog owner, and it is only natural to grieve for your beloved Frenchie. But eventually you will be able to look back on the happy memories of times spent together, and this will bring much comfort.

You may, in time, feel that your life is not complete without a French Bulldog, and you will feel ready to welcome a new puppy into your home.

Social skills

To live in the modern world, without fears and anxieties, your French Bulldog needs to receive an education in social skills so that he learns to cope calmly and confidently in a wide variety of situations. The Frenchie is an outgoing dog, with few hang-ups, and will relish the opportunity to broaden his horizons.

Early learning

The breeder will have begun a programme of socialisation by getting the puppies used to all the sights and sounds of a busy household. You need to continue this when your pup arrives in his new home, making sure he is not worried by household equipment, such as the vacuum cleaner or the washing machine, and that he gets used to unexpected noises from the radio and television.

To begin with, your puppy needs to get used to all the members of his new family (see Meeting the Family, page 84), but then you should give him the opportunity to meet friends and other people who visit your home. If you do not have children, make sure your puppy has the chance to meet and play with other people's children, making sure interactions are always supervised, so he learns that people come in small sizes, too.

The Frenchie is a sociable dog and enjoys the comings and goings of a busy household so meeting and greeting will rarely be a problem.

However, he can be pushy when it comes to getting attention and, although you may feel flattered because your Frenchie is so focused on you, it is a trait that needs to be nipped in the bud. The intelligent Frenchie can be quite manipulative, and will soon get in to the habit of demanding attention from you, rather than waiting his turn. This is most likely to occur in multi-dog households, but it can also apply to single dogs.

If you think your Frenchie is attempting to rule the roost, adopt the following strategy:

- When your Frenchie jumps up at you, demanding attention (possibly pushing other dogs out of the way), simply ignore him. Turn away and do not speak to him, even to tell him off, as he will regard this as another form of attention

- Wait until he is calm and quiet, with all four feet in the ground, and then give him the attention he craves. You will need to be completely consistent in your training and repeat this lesson continually so that your Frenchie learns that his attention-seeking strategies do not work. He will only get attention when you are ready to give it.

- If you live in a multi-dog household, feed your dogs in the same order, and when you go for a walk always put leads on in the same order. The pushy dog must never be first; he has to learn to wait his turn.

This may seem harsh, and the Frenchie is so appealing it is easy to give in to his charms. But in order to live contentedly under the same roof, a Frenchie must have respect for all members of his family – human and canine.

The outside world

When your puppy has completed his vaccinations, he is ready to venture into the outside world. French Bulldogs are generally pretty confident but there is a lot for a youngster to take on board, so do not swamp him with too many new experiences when you first set out.

Obviously you need to work at lead-training (see page 140) before you set out on your first expedition. There will be plenty of distractions to cope with, so you do not want additional problems of coping with a dog that is pulling or lagging on the lead.

Hopefully, you can set off with your Frenchie walking by your side on a loose lead. He may need additional encouragement when you venture further afield, so arm yourself with some extra special treats, which will give him a good reason to focus on you when required!

Start socialising your puppy in a quiet area with light traffic, and only progress to a busier place when he is ready. There is so much to see and hear – people (maybe carrying bags or umbrellas), pushchairs, bicycles, cars, lorries, machinery – so give your puppy a chance to take it all in.

If he does appear worried, do not fall into the trap of sympathising with him, or worse still, picking him up. This will only teach your pup that he had a good reason to be worried and, with luck, you will rescue him if he feels scared.

Instead, give him a little space so he does not have to confront whatever he is frightened of, and distract him with a few treats. Then encourage him to walk past, using an encouraging tone of voice, never forcing him by yanking on the lead.

Reward him for any forward movement, and your puppy will soon learn that he can trust you, and there is nothing to fear. Your pup also needs to continue his education in canine manners, stared by his mother and by his littermates, as he needs to be able to greet all dogs calmly, giving the signals that say he is friendly and offers no threat.

The French Bulldog is nearly always friendly in his intentions, but other dogs sometimes find it hard to read his body language. Facial expressions in brachycephalic breeds can be more limited, and the Frenchie does not have a tail of sufficient length for signalling. If you have a friend who has a dog of sound temperament, this is an ideal way to get your puppy used to social interactions. As he gets older and more established, you can widen his circle of canine acquaintances.

Training Classes

A training class will give your French Bulldog the opportunity to work alongside other dogs in a controlled situation, and he will also learn to focus on you in a different, distracting environment. Both these lessons will be vital as your dog matures.

However, the training class needs to be of the highest calibre or you risk doing more harm than good. Before you go along with your puppy, attend a class as an observer to make sure you are happy with what goes on.

Find out the following:

- How much training experience do the instructors have?
- Are the classes divided into appropriate age categories?
- Do the instructors have experience training French Bulldogs?
- Do they use positive, reward-based training methods?

If the training class is well run, it is certainly worth attending. Both you and your Frenchie will learn useful training exercises; it will increase his social skills, and you will have the chance to talk to lots of like-minded dog enthusiasts.

Training guidelines

The French Bulldog is a clever dog and is quick to learn. However, he has an independent streak which means that he may, on occasion, become more focused on following his own agenda than pleasing you!

You will be keen to get started, but in your rush to get training underway, do not neglect the fundamentals which could make the difference between success and failure.

You need to get into the mindset of a Frenchie, working out what motivates him and, equally, what makes him switch off.

Decide on your priorities for training, and then think of ways of making your training as much fun – and as positive – as possible.

When you start training, try to observe the following guidelines:

- Choose an area that is free from distractions so your puppy will focus on you. You can move on to a more challenging environment as your pup progresses.
- Do not train your puppy just after he has eaten or when you have returned from exercise. He will either be too full, or too tired, to concentrate.
- Do not train if you are in a bad mood, or if you are short of time. These sessions always end in disaster!
- Providing a worthwhile reward is an essential tool in training. This is not straightforward with a Frenchie, who is not a huge food enthusiast. You may need to find some extra special food treats, or you may do better with finding a toy your Frenchie really values.
- If you decide to use a toy, make sure it is only brought out for training sessions so that it accrues added value.
- Keep your verbal cues simple, and always use the same one for each exercise. For example, when you ask your puppy to go into the Down position, the cue is Down, not Lie Down, Get Down, or

anything else. Remember, your Frenchie does not speak English; he associates the sound of the word with the action.

- If your dog is finding an exercise difficult, break it down into small steps so it is easier to understand.
- Do not make your training sessions boring and repetitious; your Frenchie will lose concentration and will cease to co-operate.
- Do not train for too long, particularly with a young puppy, who has a very short attention span, and always end training sessions on a positive note. This does not necessarily mean getting an exercise right. If your pup is tired and making mistakes, ask him to do a simple exercise so you have the opportunity to praise and reward him. You may well find that he benefits from having a break and will make better progress next time you try.
- Above all, make training fun so you and your Frenchie enjoy spending quality time together.

First lessons

Like all puppies, a young French Bulldog will soak up new experiences like a sponge, so training should start from the time your pup arrives in his new home.

Wearing a collar

You may, or may not, want your Frenchie to wear a collar all the time.

But when he goes out in public places he will need to be on a lead, and so he should be used to the feel of a collar around his neck. The best plan is to accustom your pup to wearing a soft collar for a few minutes at a time until he gets used to it.

- Fit the collar so that you can get at least two fingers between the collar and his neck. Then have a game to distract his attention. This will work for a few moments; then he will stop, put his back leg up behind his neck and scratch away at the peculiar itchy thing which feels so odd.

- Bend down, rotate the collar, pat him on the head and distract him by playing with a toy or giving him a treat. Once he has worn the collar for a few minutes each day, he will soon ignore it and become used to it.

- Remember, never leave the collar on the puppy unsupervised, especially when he is outside in the garden, or when he is in his crate, as it is could get snagged, causing serious injury.

Walking on the lead

This is a simple exercise, but the French Bulldog is surprisingly strong for his size so it is a good idea to master the basics, and for your Frenchie to learn good lead walking manners before problems with pulling arise.

- Once your puppy is used to the collar, take him outside into your secure garden where there are no distractions.

- Attach the lead and, to begin with, allow him to wander with the lead trailing, making sure it does not become snarled up. Then pick up the lead and follow the pup where he wants to go; he needs to get used to the sensation of being attached to you.

- The next stage is to get your Frenchie to follow you, and for this you will need some treats. To give yourself the best chance of success, make sure the treats are high value – cheese, sausage or cooked liver – so your Frenchie is motivated to work with you.

- Show him you have a treat in your hand, and then encourage him to follow you. Walk a few paces, and if he is walking with you, stop and reward him. If he puts on the brakes, simply change direction and lure him with the treat.
- Next, introduce some changes of direction so your puppy is walking confidently alongside you. At this stage, introduce a verbal cue – Heel – when your puppy is in the correct position.
- You can then graduate to walking your puppy outside the home, as long as he has completed his vaccination programme, starting in quiet areas and building up to busier environments.

Training strategy

Some Frenchies decide that pulling on the lead is a good option, and, in no time, the dog is taking you for a walk.

This soon becomes an unpleasant experience, so it is important to adopt a strategy that makes your Frenchie realise there is absolutely no percentage in pulling.

- Restrict lead training to the garden in the initial stages so you are working in an environment that is free from distractions.
- Walk a few paces, being very aware of any tension on the lead. If you feel the lead tighten and your French Bulldog is attempting to get ahead of you, stop, change direction, and set off again. Your Frenchie needs to understand that pulling ahead has exactly the opposite effect to the one he wants. Rather than calling the tune, he has to co-operate with you.
- Keep a good supply of tasty treats and remember only reward – with food and with verbal praise – when he is walking on a loose lead by your side. The mistake made by many owners at this stage is to use the treats to lure the dog into position rather than rewarding him for the correct behaviour.
- Keep training sessions short, and when you are ready to venture into the outside world, do not be too ambitious to begin with. Build up the level of distraction and the duration of lead walking only when your Frenchie is consistently showing the behaviour you want.

Be generous with treats when you are training your Frenchie, but remember to deduct his food rations accordingly so he does not become overweight.

Come when called

The French Bulldog is utterly devoted to his family, but there are times when he gets distracted. There are so many enticing smells, places to explore, people and dogs to meet...

He will never stray too far away, but he may not always come back when you ask. The French Bulldog is not a disobedient dog, but recall training can become a real issue; so much so, that some Frenchie owners do not allow their dog's off-lead exercise. This is a great shame as it has a severe impact on your dog's quality of life, both in terms of restricting his exercise, and in denying him the mental stimulation he gets from investigating new places.

Your aim must be to make coming when called even more rewarding than your Frenchie's personal agenda.

This needs to be built up over a period of time, with lots of repetition so your Frenchie sees you as a fun person that is always ready to reward him, rather than as an irate owner who is trying to spoil his fun.

- Hopefully, the breeder will have laid the foundations simply by calling the puppies to 'Come' when it is dinnertime, or when they are moving from one place to another.
- You can build on this when your puppy arrives in his new home, calling him to 'Come' when he is in a confined space, such as the kitchen. This is a good place to build up a positive association with the verbal cue – particularly if you ask your puppy to 'Come' to get his dinner!
- The next stage is to transfer the lesson to the garden. Arm yourself with some treats, and wait until your puppy is distracted. Then call him, using a higher-pitched, excited tone of voice. At this stage, a puppy wants to be with you, so capitalise on this and keep practising the verbal cue, and rewarding your puppy with a treat and lots of praise when he comes to you.
- Now you are ready to introduce some distractions. Try calling him when someone else is in the garden, or wait a few minutes until he is investigating a really interesting scent. When

he responds, make a really big fuss of him and give him extra treats so he knows it is worth his while to come to you. If your puppy responds, immediately reward him with a treat.

- If he is slow to come, run away a few steps and then call again, making yourself sound really exciting. Jump up and down, open your arms wide to welcome him; it doesn't matter how silly you look, he needs to see you as the most fun person in the world.
- When you have a reliable recall in the garden, you can venture into the outside world. Do not be too ambitious to begin with; try a recall on a quiet place with the minimum of distractions so you can be more certain of success.
- Do not make the mistake of only asking your dog to come at the end of his allotted exercise period. What is the incentive in coming back to you if all you do is clip on his lead, marking the end of his free time? Instead, call your dog at random times, giving him a treat and a stroke, and then letting him go free again. In this way, coming to you – and focusing on you – is always rewarding.

Stationary exercises

The Sit and Down are easy to teach, and mastering these exercises will be rewarding for both you and your French Bulldog. The Frenchie can be quite excitable, so it is useful if you have a means of bringing proceedings to a standstill before everyone gets carried away!

Sit

The best method is to lure your French Bulldog into position, and for this you can use a treat or his food bowl.

- Hold the reward (a treat or food bowl) above his head. As he looks up, he will lower his hindquarters and go into a sit.
- Practise this a few times and once your puppy understands what you are asking, introduce the

verbal cue, sit. When your Frenchie understands the exercise, he will respond to the verbal cue alone, and you will not need to reward him every time he sits. However, it is a good idea to give him a treat on a random basis when he co-operates to keep him guessing!

Down

This is an important lesson, and can be a lifesaver if an emergency arises and you need to bring your French Bulldog to an instant halt.

- You can start with your dog in a Sit or a Stand for this exercise. Stand or kneel in front of him and show him you have a treat in your hand. Hold the treat just in front of his nose and slowly lower it towards the ground, between his front legs.

- As your Frenchie follows the treat he will go down on his front legs and, in a few moments, his hindquarters will follow. Close your hand over the treat so he doesn't cheat and get the treat before he is in the correct position. As soon as he is in the Down, give him the treat and lots of praise.

- Keep practising, and when your Frenchie understands what you want, introduce the verbal cue Down.

Control exercises

These exercises are not the most exciting, but they are important in establishing a relationship of mutual respect with your French Bulldog.

Wait

This exercise teaches your Frenchie to wait in position until you give the next command; it differs from the Stay exercise where he must stay where you have left him for a more prolonged period. The most useful application of Wait is when you are getting your dog out of the car and you need him to stay in position until you clip on his lead.

- Start with your puppy on the lead to give you a greater chance of success. Ask him to sit, and stand in front him. Step back one pace, holding your hand, palm flat, facing him. Wait a second and then come back to stand in front of him.

- You can then reward him and release him with a word, such as OK.
- Practise this a few times, waiting a little longer before you reward him, and then introduce the verbal cue Wait.
- You can reinforce the lesson by using it in different situations, such as asking your Frenchie to Wait before you put his food bowl down.

Stay

You need to differentiate this exercise from the Wait by using a different hand signal and a different verbal cue.

- Start with your French Bulldog in the Down as he is most likely to be secure in this position. Stand by his side and then step forwards, with your hand held back, palm facing the dog.
- Step back, release him, and then reward him. Practise until your Frenchie understands the exercise and then introduce the verbal cue Stay.
- Gradually increase the distance you can leave your puppy, and increase the challenge by walking around him – and even stepping over him – so that he learns he must stay until you release him.

Leave

A response to this verbal cue means that your French Bulldog will learn to give up a toy on request, and it follows on that he will give up anything when he is asked, which is very useful if he has got hold of a forbidden object. This is a very important for the French Bulldog who has a tendency to become possessive over things he values. It is not simply a matter of obeying the verbal cue to Leave; it is establishing the status quo, in which you are the decision-maker and your Frenchie is ready to co-operate with you.

- The Leave command can be taught quite easily when you are first playing with your puppy. As you, gently, take a toy from his mouth, introduce the verbal cue, Leave, and then praise him.
- If he is reluctant, swap the toy for another toy or a treat. This will usually do the trick.
- Do not try to pull the toy from his mouth if he refuses to give it up, as you will make the situation confrontational. Let the toy go dead in your hand, and then swap it for a new toy, or a really high-value treat, so this becomes the better option.
- Remember to make a big fuss of your Frenchie when he does as you ask.

Opportunities for French Bulldogs

The French Bulldog is an intelligent and adaptable dog, but there are limitations when it comes to competing in some of the canine sports.

Few Frenchies (or their owners!) have an appetite for rigorous training, and most French Bulldogs get bored very quickly if they are asked to do something too often. The best plan is to focus on having fun with your Frenchie and, who knows, you may even surprise yourselves...

Good Citizen Scheme

The Kennel Club Good Citizen Scheme was introduced to promote responsible dog ownership, and to teach dogs basic good manners. In the

US there is one test; in the UK there are four award levels: Puppy Foundation, Bronze, Silver and Gold.

Exercises within the scheme include:

- Walking on lead
- Road walking
- Control at door/gate.
- Food manners
- Recall
- Stay
- Send to bed
- Emergency stop.

Obedience

If your French Bulldog has mastered basic obedience, you may want to get involved in competitive obedience.

The exercises include: heelwork at varying paces, with dog and handler following a pattern decided by the judge, stays, recalls, retrieves, sendaways, scent discrimination and distance control. The exercises get progressively harder as you progress up the classes. A Frenchie will readily learn the exercises that are used in obedience competitions, but this is a discipline that calls for a very high degree of precision and accuracy which does not suit all dogs, or all handlers.

Rally O

If you do not want to get involved in the rigours of Competitive Obedience, you may find that a sport called Rally O is more to your liking.

This is loosely based on Obedience, and also has a few exercises borrowed from Agility (see below) when you get to the highest levels. Handler and dog must complete a course, in the designated order, which has a variety of up to 20 different exercises. The course is timed and the team must complete within the time limit that is set, but there are no bonus marks for speed.

The great advantage of Rally O is that it is very relaxed, and anyone can compete; indeed, it has proved very popular for handlers with disabilities, as they are able to work their dogs to a high standard and compete on equal terms.

Agility

The French Bulldog is small and powerful but he should also be active, so Agility is a sport worth considering. This involves the dog completing an obstacle course under the guidance of his owner. You need a good element of control with this sport, as the dog competes off the lead. In competition, each dog is assessed on both time and accuracy. The dog that completes the course in the fastest time, with the fewest faults, wins the class. The obstacles include an A-frame, a dog-walk, weaving poles, a see-saw, tunnels, and jumps.

Showing

Exhibiting a dog in the show ring sounds easy but, in fact, it entails a lot of training and preparation, particularly when you are asking a strong-minded, breed to compete in a beauty competition.

Your French Bulldog will have to be calm and confident in the busy show atmosphere, so you need to work on his socialisation, and also take him to ringcraft classes so you both learn what is required in the ring. Your Frenchie will be subjected to a detailed hands-on examination by the judge; he must learn to stand still in a show pose and to move on a loose lead so the judge can assess his gait. Showing at the top level is highly addictive, so watch out, once you start, you will never have a free date in your diary!

Frenchies love to show off, so why not teach your dog some tricks so he can entertain visitors when they come round!

Health care

We are fortunate that the French Bulldog is a healthy breed and, with good routine care, a well balanced diet, and sufficent exercise, most will experience few health problems.

However, it is your responsibility to put a programme of preventative health care in place, and this should start from the moment your puppy, or older dog, arrives in his new home.

Vaccinations

Dogs are subject to a number of contagious diseases. In the old days, these were killers, and resulted in heartbreak for many owners.

Vaccinations have now been developed, and the occurrence of the major infectious diseases is now very rare. However, this will only remain the case if all pet owners follow a strict policy of vaccinating their dogs.

There are vaccinations available for the following diseases:

Adenovirus: (Canine Adenovirus) This attacks the liver and affected dogs have a classic 'blue eye'.

Distemper: A viral disease which causes chest and gastro-intestinal damage. The brain may also be affected, leading to fits and paralysis.

Parvovirus: Causes severe gastro enteritis, and most commonly affects puppies.

Leptospirosis: This bacterial disease is carried by rats and affects many mammals, including humans. It causes liver and kidney damage.

Rabies: A virus that affects the nervous system and is invariably fatal. The first signs are abnormal behavior when the infected dog may bite another animal or a person. Paralysis and death follow. Vaccination is compulsory in most countries. In the UK, dogs travelling overseas must be vaccinated.

Kennel Cough: There are several strains of Kennel Cough, but they all result in a harsh, dry, cough. This disease is rarely fatal; in fact most dogs make a good recovery within a matter of weeks and show few signs of ill health while they are affected. However, kennel cough is highly infectious among dogs that live together so, for this reason, most boarding kennels will insist that your dog is protected by the vaccine, which is given as nose drops.

Lyme disease: This is a bacterial disease transmitted by ticks (see page 171). The first signs are limping, but the heart, kidneys and nervous system can also be affected. The ticks that transmit the disease occur in specific regions, such as the north-east states of the USA, some of the southern states, California and the upper Mississippi region. Lyme disease is still rare in the UK so vaccinations are not routinely offered.

Vaccination programme

In the USA, the American Animal Hospital Association advises vaccination for core diseases, which they list as distemper, adenovirus, parvovirus and rabies. The requirement for vaccinating for non-core diseases – leptospriosis, Lyme disease and kennel cough – should be assessed depending on a dog's individual risk and his likely exposure to the disease.

In the UK, vaccinations are routinely given for distemper, adenovirus, leptospirosis and parvovirus. In most cases, a puppy will start his vaccinations at around eight weeks of age, with the second part given a fortnight later. However, this does vary depending on the individual policy of veterinary practices, and the incidence of disease in your area.

You should also talk to your vet about whether to give annual booster vaccinations. This depends on an individual dog's levels of immunity, and how long a particular vaccine remains effective.

Parasites

No matter how well you look after your French Bulldog, you will have to accept that parasites (internal and external) are ever present, and you need to take preventative action.

Preventative treatment is essential for the control of both internal and external parasites.

Internal parasites: As the name suggests, these parasites live inside your dog. Most will find a home in the digestive tract, but there is also a parasite that lives in the heart. If infestation is unchecked, a dog's health will be severely jeopardised, but routine preventative treatment is simple and effective.

External parasites: These parasites live on your dog's body – in his skin and fur, and sometimes in his ears.

Roundworm

This is found in the small intestine, and signs of infestation will be a poor coat, a pot belly, diarrhoea and lethargy. Pregnant mothers should be treated, but it is almost inevitable that parasites will be passed on to the puppies. For this reason, a breeder will start a worming programme, which you will need to continue. Ask your vet for advice on treatment, which will be ongoing throughout your dog's life.

Tapeworm

Infection occurs when fleas and lice are ingested; the adult worm takes up residence in the small intestine, releasing mobile segments (which contain eggs) that can be seen in a dog's faeces as small rice-like grains. The only other obvious sign of infestation is irritation of the anus. Again, routine preventative treatment is required throughout your Frenchie's life.

Heartworm

This parasite is transmitted by mosquitoes, and so will only occur where these insects thrive. A warm environment is needed for the parasite to develop, so it is more likely to be present in areas with a warm, humid climate. However, it is found in all parts of the USA, although its prevalence does vary. At present, heartworm is rarely seen in the UK.

Heartworm live in the right side of the heart. Larvae can grow up to 14 inches (35.5cm) in length. A dog with heartworm is at severe risk from heart failure, so preventative treatment, as advised by your vet, is essential. Dogs living in the USA should have regular blood tests to check for the presence of infection.

Lungworm

Lungworm, or *Angiostrongylus vasorum*, is a parasite that lives in the heart and major blood vessels supplying the lungs. It can cause many problems, such as breathing difficulties, blood-clotting problems, sickness and diarrhoea, seizures, and can be fatal. The parasite is carried by slugs and snails, and the dog becomes infected when ingesting these, often accidentally when rummaging through undergrowth. Lungworm is not common, but it is on the increase and a responsible owner should be aware of it. Fortunately, it is easily preventable and even affected dogs usually make a full recovery if treated early enough. Your vet will be able to advise you on the risks in your area and what form of treatment may be required

Fleas

A dog may carry dog fleas, cat fleas, and even human fleas. The flea stays on the dog only long enough to have a blood meal and to breed, but its presence will result in itching and scratching. If your dog has an allergy to fleas, which is usually a reaction to the flea's saliva, he will scratch himself until he is raw.

How to detect fleas

You may suspect your dog has fleas, but how can you be sure? There are two methods to try.

Run a fine comb through your dog's coat, and see if you can detect the presence of fleas on the skin, or clinging to the comb. Alternatively, sit your dog on white paper and rub his back. This will dislodge faeces from the fleas, which will be visible as small brown specks. To double check, shake the specks on to damp cotton-wool (cotton). Flea faeces consists of the dried blood taken from the host, so if the specks turn a lighter shade of red, you know your dog has fleas.

Spot-on treatment administered on a routine basis is easy to use and highly effective on all types of fleas. You can also treat your dog with a spray or with insecticidal shampoo. Bear in mind that the whole environment your dog lives in will need to be sprayed, and all other pets living in your home will also need to be treated.

Ticks

These are blood-sucking parasites which are most frequently found in rural areas where sheep or deer are present. The main danger is their ability to pass Lyme disease to both dogs and humans. Lyme disease is prevalent in some areas of the USA (see page 165), although it is still rare in the UK.

The treatment you give your dog for fleas generally works for ticks, but you should discuss the best product to use with your vet.

How to remove a tick

If you spot a tick on your dog, do not try to pluck it off as you risk leaving the hard mouth parts embedded in his skin. The best way to remove a tick is to use a fine pair of tweezers, or you can buy a tick remover. Grasp the tick head firmly and then pull the tick straight out from the skin. If you are using a tick remover, check the instructions, as some recommend a circular twist when pulling. When you have removed the tick, clean the area with mild soap and water.

Ear mites

These parasites live in the outer ear canal. The signs of infestation are a brown, waxy discharge, and your dog will continually shake his head and scratch his ear.

If you suspect your French Bulldog has ear mites, a visit to the vet will be needed so that medicated ear drops can be prescribed.

Fur mites

These small, white parasites are visible to the naked eye and are often referred to as 'walking dandruff'.

They cause a scurfy coat and mild itchiness. However, they are zoonetic – transferable to humans – so prompt treatment with an insecticide prescribed by your vet is essential.

Harvest mites

These are picked up from the undergrowth, and can be seen as a bright orange patch on the webbing between the toes, although this can be found elsewhere on the body, such as on the ears flaps. Treatment is effective with the appropriate insecticide.

Skin mites

There are two types of parasite that burrow into a dog's skin. Demodex canis is transferred from a mother to her pups while they are feeding. Treatment is with a topical preparation, and sometimes antibiotics are needed.

The other skin mite is *Sarcoptes scabiei*, which causes intense itching and hair loss. It is highly contagious, so all dogs in a household will need to be treated, which involves repeated bathing with a medicated shampoo.

Common ailments

As with all living animals, dogs can be affected by a variety of ailments. Most can be treated effectively after consulting with your vet, who will prescribe appropriate medication and will advise you on how to care for your dog's needs.

Here are some of the more common problems that could affect your French Bulldog, with advice on how to deal with them.

Anal glands

These are two small sacs on either side of the anus, which produce a dark-brown secretion that dogs use when they mark their territory. The anal glands should empty every time a dog defecates but if they become blocked or impacted, a dog will experience increasing discomfort. He may nibble at his rear end,

or scoot his bottom along the ground to relieve the irritation. Treatment involves a trip to the vet, who will empty the glands manually. It is important to do this without delay or infection may occur.

Dental problems

Good dental hygiene will do much to minimise gum infection and tooth decay, which is why teeth cleaning should be part of your regular care routine. If tartar accumulates to the extent that you cannot remove it by brushing, the vet will need to intervene. In a situation such as this, an anaesthetic will need to be administered so the tartar can be removed manually.

Diarrhoea

There are many reasons why a dog has diarrhoea, but most commonly it is the result of scavenging, a sudden change of diet, or an adverse reaction to a particular type of food.

If your dog is suffering from diarrhoea, the first step is to withdraw food for a day. It is important that he does not dehydrate, so make sure that fresh drinking water is available. However, drinking too much can increase the diarrhoea, which may be accompanied by vomiting, so limit how much he drinks at any one time.

After allowing the stomach to rest, feed a bland diet, such as white fish or chicken with boiled rice, for a few days. In most cases, your dog's motions will return to normal and you can resume usual feeding, although this should be done gradually.

However, if this fails to work and the diarrhoea persists for more than a few days, you should consult you vet. Your dog may have an infection which needs to be treated with antibiotics, or the diarrhoea may indicate some other problem which needs expert diagnosis.

Ear infections

The French Bulldog has erect ears which allow the air to circulate freely, thus minimising the risk of ear infections. A healthy ear is clean with no sign of redness or inflammation, and no evidence of a waxy brown discharge or a foul odour. If you see your dog scratching his ear, shaking his head, or holding one ear at an odd angle, you will need to consult your vet.

The most likely causes are ear mites, an infection, or there may a foreign body, such as a grass seed, trapped in the ear. Depending on the cause, treatment is with medicated ear drops, possibly containing antibiotics. If a foreign body is suspected, the vet will need to carry our further investigations.

Eye problems

The French Bulldog has round eyes which should not be sunken nor prominent. This lack of exaggeration means that a Frenchie's eyes should not be predisposed to infection or vulnerable to injury or trauma, which is the case with breeds such as the Pekingese, which have somewhat bulging eyes.

However, there is tendency towards more prominent eyes in the breed, and this can lead to problems such as corneal ulcers (see page 186).

If your French Bulldog's eyes look red and sore, he may be suffering from conjunctivitis. This may, or may not be accompanied with a watery or a crusty discharge. Conjunctivitis can be caused by a bacterial or viral infection, it could be the result of an injury, or it could be an adverse reaction to pollen.

You will need to consult your vet for a correct diagnosis, but in the case of an infection, treatment with medicated eye drops is effective.

Conjunctivitis may also be the first sign of more serious inherited eye problems (see page 186).

Heatstroke

The French Bulldog has a flat, upturned nose, and although the nostrils should be open to allow for normal breathing, it is inevitable that breathing is more laboured in the brachycephalic breeds, and they are therefore more likely to suffer from over-heating.

In its mildest form this causes discomfort, but if a Frenchie's body temperature is allowed to rise so that he is suffering from heatstroke, the consequences can be disastrous.

This is particularly the case if your Frenchie is affected by brachycephalic airway obstruction, see page 184.

If the weather is warm, make sure your French Bulldog has access to shady areas, and wait for a cooler part of the day before going for a walk.

Be extra careful if you leave your Frenchie in the car as the temperature can rise dramatically – even on a cloudy day. Heatstroke can happen very rapidly, and unless you are able lower your dog's temperature, it can be fatal.

If your dog appears to be suffering from heatstroke, lie him flat and work at lowering his temperature by spraying him with cool water and covering him with wet towels.

As soon as he has made some recovery, take him to the vet, where cold intravenous fluids can be administered.

Lameness/limping

There are a wide variety of reasons why a dog can go lame, from a simple muscle strain, to a fracture, ligament damage, or more complex problems with the joints.

If you are concerned about your dog, do not delay in seeking help. It will help if you ensure his bed is in a warm draught-free location, and if your Frenchie gets wet after exercise, you must dry him thoroughly.

If your Frenchie seems to be in pain, consult your vet who will be able to help with pain relief medication.

Skin problems

If your dog is scratching or nibbling at his skin, first check he is free from fleas (see page 170).

There are other external parasites which cause itching and hair loss, but you will need a vet to help you find the culprit.

An allergic reaction is another major cause of skin problems. It can be quite an undertaking to find the cause of the allergy, and you will need to follow your vet's advice, which often requires eliminating specific ingredients from the diet, as well as looking at environmental factors.

Breed-specific disorders

Like all pedigree dogs, the French Bulldog does have some breed-related disorders. If diagnosed with any of the diseases listed here, it is important to remember that they can affect offspring so breeding from such dogs should be discouraged.

There are now recognised screening tests to enable breeders to check for affected individuals and hence reduce the prevalence of these diseases within the breed.

DNA testing is also becoming more widely available, and as research into the different genetic diseases progresses, more DNA tests are being developed.

Brachycephalic Airway Obstruction Syndrome

Brachycephalic breeds, such as the French Bulldog, are predisposed to this condition because of their head construction which can lead to defects such as an elongated soft palate, narrowed nostrils, abnormalities of the larynx, and/or a narrow windpipe. Minor signs are snuffling and snorting, progressing to intolerance to exercise and breathing difficulties, with collapse in its most severe form.

Prevention in terms of guarding against over-exertion and over-heating is vital for affected dogs. Surgery, which is high-risk for dogs with this condition, can be used to shorten an elongated soft palate.

Colitis, Histiocytic Ulcerative

There appears to be a breed tendency towards this form of inflammatory bowel disease, which appears in young dogs, often less than 12 months of age. Typical signs are weight loss, poor growth and frequent straining to pass loose, mucoid faeces, which may contain fresh blood. Additional signs include periods of constipation, vomiting, lethargy and poor appetite. Treatment involves drugs to suppress the immune system and dietary manipulation.

Deafness

It is primarily white dogs, in many breeds, that have a higher incidence of deafness. This means that pied French Bulldogs are more likely to be affected. Hearing can be assessed through BAER testing, when puppies are around six weeks of age, and all affected dogs should be excluded from breeding programmes.

Eye disorders

Chronic Superficial Keratitis

Also so known as Pannus, this involves long-term inflammation of the cornea, often accompanied by conjunctivitis. Treatment with eye drops controls and slows the progress of the condition, but is it essentially irreversible and eventually results in blindness.

Corneal ulcers

This is generally caused by an irritation on the cornea, and French Bulldogs who have prominent eyes are more likely to be affected.

Treatment with eye drops is effective, particularly if administered before the condition deteriorates. In severe cases, surgery may be required to aid healing.

Entropion

This is an inherited eye condition which presents as an in-rolling of the eyelids.

This ranges in severity from mild to the more serious, where surgical correction is required because of the pain and damage that is inflicted on the eyeball.

Hereditary cataracts

Cataracts are an opacification of the lens that tends to occur in older dogs. There are varying degrees of severity, the inherited form often having little effect on eyesight but, if necessary, surgery is usually a successful treatment.

Hemivertebrae

The vertebrae are the building blocks of the bony spine, designed to protect the spinal cord as it runs from the underside of the brain down the length

of the back. In this condition, the vertebrae are misshapen or deformed and cannot, therefore, fulfil their protective function.

The effect depends on which vertebrae are affected, varying from kinking of the spinal column, hind limb weakness, or, at worst, paralysis. Surgery may be possible in some cases.

It has been found that puppies with very short bodies are more likely to be affected, and it is essential that all potential breeding stock is thoroughly assessed, using X-rays if necessary

Patellar luxation

This is where the kneecap or patella slips out of position, locking the knee or stifle so that it will not bend.

Characteristically the affected dog will hop for a couple of paces until the patella slips back into its correct position over the stifle joint.

Most dogs live with this condition but in severe cases, surgery may be the best option.

Summing up

It may give the pet owner cause for concern to find about health problems that may affect their dog. But it is important to bear in mind that acquiring some basic knowledge is an asset, as it will allow you to spot signs of trouble at an early stage. Early diagnosis is very often the means to the most effective treatment.

Fortunately, the French Bulldog is a generally healthy and disease-free dog, with his only visits to the vet being annual check-ups. In most cases, owners can look forward to enjoying many happy years with this affectionate and highly entertaining companion.

Useful addresses

Breed & Kennel Clubs

Please contact your Kennel Club to obtain contact information about breed clubs in your area.

UK

The Kennel Club (UK)
1 Clarges Street London, W1J 8AB
Telephone: 0870 606 6750
Fax: 0207 518 1058
Web: www.thekennelclub.org.uk

USA

American Kennel Club (AKC)
5580 Centerview Drive, Raleigh, NC 27606.
Telephone: 919 233 9767
Fax: 919 233 3627
Email: info@akc.org
Web: www.akc.org

United Kennel Club (UKC)
100 E Kilgore Rd, Kalamazoo,
MI 49002-5584, USA.
Tel: 269 343 9020
Fax: 269 343 7037
Web: www.ukcdogs.com

Australia

Australian National Kennel Council (ANKC)
The Australian National Kennel Council is the administrative body for pure breed canine affairs in Australia. It does not, however, deal directly with dog exhibitors, breeders or judges. For information pertaining to breeders, clubs or shows, please contact the relevant State or Territory Body.

International

Fédération Cynologique Internationalé (FCI)
Place Albert 1er, 13, B-6530 Thuin, Belgium.
Tel: +32 71 59.12.38
Fax: +32 71 59.22.29
Web: www.fci.be

Training and behavior

UK

Association of Pet Dog Trainers
Telephone: 01285 810811
Web: www.apdt.co.uk

Canine Behaviour
Association of Pet Behaviour Counsellors
Telephone: 01386 751151
Web: www.apbc.org.uk

USA

Association of Pet Dog Trainers
Tel: 1 800 738 3647
Web: www.apdt.com

American College of Veterinary Behaviorists
Web: dacvb.org

American Veterinary Society of Animal Behavior
Web: www.avsabonline.org

Australia

APDT Australia Inc
Web: www.apdt.com.au

For details of regional behaviorists, contact the relevant State or Territory Controlling Body.

Activities

UK

Agility Club
www.agilityclub.co.uk

British Flyball Association
Telephone: 01628 829623
Web: www.flyball.org.uk

USA

North American Dog Agility Council
Web: www.nadac.com

North American Flyball Association, Inc.
Tel/Fax: 800 318 6312
Web: www.flyball.org

Australia

Agility Dog Association of Australia
Tel: 0423 138 914
Web: www.adaa.com.au

NADAC Australia
Web: www.nadacaustralia.com

Australian Flyball Association
Tel: 0407 337 939
Web: www.flyball.org.au

International

World Canine Freestyle Organisation
Tel: (718) 332-8336
Web: www.worldcaninefreestyle.org

Health

UK

British Small Animal Veterinary Association
Tel: 01452 726700
Web: www.bsava.com

Royal College of Veterinary Surgeons
Tel: 0207 222 2001
Web: www.rcvs.org.uk

www.dogbooksonline.co.uk/healthcare

Alternative Veterinary Medicine Centre
Tel: 01367 710324
Web: www.alternativevet.org

USA

American Veterinary Medical Association
Tel: 800 248 2862
Web: www.avma.org

American College of Veterinary Surgeons
Tel: 301 916 0200
Toll Free: 877 217 2287
Web: www.acvs.org

Canine Eye Registration Foundation
The Veterinary Medical DataBases
1717 Philo Rd, PO Box 3007,
Urbana, IL 61803-3007
Tel: 217-693-4800
Fax: 217-693-4801
Web: www.vmdb.org/cerf.html

Orthopaedic Foundation of Animals
2300 E Nifong Boulevard
Columbia, Missouri, 65201-3806
Tel: 573 442-0418
Fax: 573 875-5073
Web: www.offa.org

American Holistic Veterinary Medical Association
Tel: 410 569 0795
Web: www.ahvma.org

Australia

Australian Small Animal Veterinary Association
Tel: 02 9431 5090
Web: www.asava.com.au

Australian Veterinary Association
Tel: 02 9431 5000
Web: www.ava.com.au

Australian College Veterinary Scientists
Tel: 07 3423 2016
Web: acvsc.org.au

Australian Holistic Vets
Web: www.ahv.com.au